The 7 Skills of the ancien

Discover how the 7 skills of Disci

and enable you to leave a lastin

Donald G. Doty, Ph.D.

Companion video based Website link:

http://thediscipleshiplab.com/

ᛃ Dedication ᛩ

To my love Patty Elizabeth and
my two first disciples, Jake and Dusty

ᛃ Selected Testimonials from Leaders

who have experienced the power of Discipleship ᛩ

"I would give the teachings a 7 in terms of added value to in my work life and contributed to my development in my work leadership style. The readings and assignments in regards to modeling and storytelling also contributed greatly to my learning."   K.P. , Director of Branches/North Region| Sound Credit Union

"In regards to leadership skills improvement, I would have to give you a "10" (7 is not high enough). These teachings with the emphasis on serving people, is exactly what I needed. Prior to this, I did not know it, but I was sabotaging myself at work with my own leadership style. Now I am actively mentoring a replacement and have built a team of people that genuinely enjoy each other. It now looks like I am going to receive a promotion this summer in which I will go from leading inventory team members for about 1/2 a hospital to leading inventory team members for 9 hospitals. Your tremendous teachings have changed my life and my heart in ways that defy personality assessment probabilities."   J.B., V.P., Providence Hospital

"I assumed people by nature, were leaders or followers, and anything in between was a waste of biological ingenuity. That is not to say that people could not learn to lead, I just assumed that a heavy dose of charisma is what truly defined great leadership. It is with this understanding that I thought charisma was the differentiating factor between poor companies and great companies. Your teachings have shown me how misguided I have been, and given me a new perspective on leadership. I do not believe that leaders are influenced or defined by the charismatic brevity of life, but by being masters of apprenticeship and discipleship." J.J., U.S. Army

Table of Contents

1

The Value of the Ancient Paradigm of Discipleship

"Give a man a fish; you have fed him for today.

Teach a man to fish; and you have fed him for a lifetime"

"Greed is good!" said Gordon Gekko (Michael Douglas) in Oliver Stone's

gripping movie Wall Street. After glimpsing the financial devastation that resulted from such a mantra, Gecko's protégé Bud Fox (Charlie Sheen) asked a very telling question, "So where does it all end, Gordon? How much is enough?" "It's not a question of enough, pal," replied Gekko. And then he let the kid in on his secret philosophy, his personal prescription for success: "Money itself isn't lost or made, it's simply…uh, *transferred*, from one perception to another. Like magic." Gekko then pointed out an elaborate impressionistic painting on his office wall. "This painting here," he said, "I bought it 10 years ago for sixty thousand dollars. I could sell it today for six hundred thousand. The illusion has become real. And the more real it becomes, the more desperately they want it." Then, to emphasize the importance of this lesson he remarked with a smirk in amazement, "What I do, stocks and real estate speculation….It's bull---!" Gekko then revealed the real dirty little secret that underpinned his philosophy, "I create nothing!"

Who knew how pertinent Gekko's words would be for us today? Financial markets driven by greed and Madoff ponzi schemes, WaMu-like mortgage lending with zero security, and Enron size balance sheet overstatements. Billions of dollars have now been spent in attempts to rectify this horrid situation- leaving a public disillusioned and burdened with a huge amount of debt and mistrust. Corporate and government executives who break the public trust should swap their pin stripe suits for horizontally striped prison garb. But can legislation alone correct corruption? Federal regulations and organizational ethics mantras may act as boundaries to behavior in commerce. But as the past two several decades of fraud and accounting scandals have demonstrated, they are powerless to constrain the few powerful, but undisciplined, individuals from making mistakes that put the public good at risk. As George Washington said, "Few men have virtue to withstand the highest bidder."

There still appears to be significant need for improvement. Many retailing "household name" companies like J.C. Penney, Montgomery Ward, and Sears are failing. And only one of the companies originally listed on the Dow Jones Industrials is still in existence, General Electric. Bass's review of several decades of leadership studies showed that little basic research exists which explains how the mechanisms of leadership paradigms actually work in skill development and organizational performance. As a recent example, while Google's 2012 Oxygen project assessed the relationship between leadership attributes and employee satisfaction measures, effects of leadership on more mission centric measures such as sales and productivity were not substantiated (See "How Google sold its engineers on management," by David A. Garvin, HBR December 2013). According recent Small Business Administration statistics, the rate of small business failure has not significantly improved from the last Census in 2000, averaging around 50% after 5 years as shown in the Figure below, no better than chance.

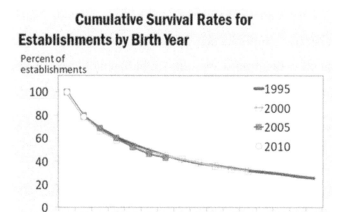

Cumulative Survival Rates for Establishments by Birth Year

Source: Bureau of Labor Statistics, BED.

What's in it for you?

If you would like to change your world, your business or organization, or alter a troubling trend in your family line, *to influence people in such a way that your legacy will live generations after you pass away*- this book is for you. You may be a CEO who wants to grow a strong bench for the company, a coach who wants to build a winning team for this season and the next- an arts or music professional whose style and performance should not end at the end of his or her career- a school teacher who has a classroom full of potential lives to be influenced- a board member who really believes in an organization and wants to secure its future- a family business person who is about to retire and wants the business he or she built to endure and prosper, a physician who desires to pass knowledge on to budding medical interns- or a parent or grandparent who simply wants to pass on their most important values or ideals to your (grand) children to change their future.

An estimated 78.2 million baby boomers in the United States alone are about to retire and to pass the baton of leadership to the next generation. If you are one of them you're probably wondering... How will my hand off to the leaders of the future go? How well will the next generation do as stewards of the resources (money, talent, time) that has been invested in them? The lessons herein can grow people's skills, but also moral values and sound character that can be passed on to future generations. This book is written for people who want their impact and influence *to last beyond their lifetimes-* who want to influence not just their immediate family or staff, but to create *generations and generations* of extraordinary people who will follow them. If you are that kind of person, or would like to learn how to become one, this book is for you.

Over the past 50 years, hundreds of books have been written on the leadership of people - Blanchard's 1 Minute Manager, Deming's 14 points for management, Drucker's Management by Objectives, Myers-Briggs personality typologies, Senge's Learning Organizations and others. All of these have had limited success and application "in their day", but few have provided a durable heuristic to explain how people can sustain great performance over long periods time. Most of these leadership, mentoring, or training texts written over the last century have utilized a "teach a man to fish, and you have fed him for a lifetime" paradigm. They've focused on teaching best practices and leadership skills informed by the notion that by teaching a man to fish, you have enabled him to feed himself. This was all well and good in a time where fish, competing fishermen, and rivers where one could find fish were relatively stable.

However, in today's torrid pace of change, diversity of human resources, and globally competitive industries the "teach a man to fish" paradigm is increasingly ineffective. *Herein, you'll discover how the ancient paradigm or "map" of discipleship can enable you to turn ordinary people into extraordinary ones.* The discipleship paradigm is designed to a "teach a man to fish *and how to mentor another* in the art and science of fishing", in a sustainable fashion. In this way leaders like you may be enabled to pass on knowledge and influence the character of their followers, and to influence multiple generations into the future.

Discipleship, an Ancient Paradigm with "Pass it On" Promise

How then can you bring lasting change to your world? By building character and skill in the life of one person at a time. Then by enabling them to "pass it on"- to build the character and skill of another, and another, and so on. This sounds good in theory. But as shown by multiple failures of leadership it appears to be easier said than done. Fortunately, a time tested model for building character and skill offers promise. *This model is found in the ancient paradigm of discipleship.* The discipleship paradigm appears to be more powerful than authentic, transactional or even transformational leadership paradigms[1]. In authentic leadership leaders lead simply and are genuinely themselves in all situations.

While authenticity may inspire trust and followership to some degree, no reliable linkage has been found to sustainability of organizational performance over time. In transactional leadership, the focus is on "tit for tat" or compensation for tasks performed. For example, one might pay a construction worker $200 per square foot of finished space, the focus is on the *transaction*. Transformational leadership is slightly better. The leader works to transform a person's skill, attitudes, and performance.

Transformational leadership is akin a "teaching a man to fish" analogy. The focus of the leader is to *transform the person to produce good results.* Discipleship goes beyond these two paradigms. Through the ancient paradigm of discipleship, people are transformed and productive tasks result. But discipleship doesn't stop there. The focus is both to enable *transformation of the person,* and to teach that individual how to transform others, who in turn, can transform others, generation after generation. Discipleship can turn ordinary people into extraordinary ones. How the 3 models of leadership compare in influencing multiple generations sustainably over time are shown below:

Paradigm	Result	Number of People influenced
Transactional	Productive Tasks get done	(1 figure)
Transformational	Productive Tasks, Skills	(1 figure)
Discipleship	Productivity plus teaching others	(1 figure) (3 figures) (4 figures) (5 figures) ...

What is discipleship? Discipleship may be seen through the mentor-protégé success stories that resound through the centuries from all walks of life. Socrates and Plato, Plato and Aristotle, Aristotle and Alexander the Great, Archimedes and Galileo, Christian Gottlieb Neefe and Ludwig van Beethoven, Camille Pissaro and Paul Cezanne, Ezra Pound and T. S. Eliot, Bourke Cochran and Winston Churchill, Sir Keith Joseph and Margaret Thatcher, Anne Sullivan and Helen Keller, Major General Fox Connor and Dwight David Eisenhower, Benjamin Mays and Martin Luthe r King, Jr., Zhuge Liang and Jiang Wei, Gertrude Stein and Ernest Hemingway, Kau Sze and Grandmaster Chan Sau Chung, Sir Laurence Olivier and Anthony Hopkins, Bill Walsh and Bill Belechick.

What do all these ordinary people who became extraordinary have in common? These famous pairs of people experienced the wonderful chemistry of a relationship in which they were mentored to extraordinary greatness in both character and performance. There is a wonderful saying, "the wise elders planted trees, the fruit of which they knew they would enjoy for generation after generation." Unfortunately, people who have experienced this kind of mentored pairing and success are in the minority. Consider the lack of continuity and success of family businesses[2]. In the United States small businesses generate over 40-60% of the gross national product. Yet only about 50% survive after 5 years according to the U.S. Small Business Administration. In India, it is estimated that over 80% of the GNP is attributed to family businesses. However, less than one-third of Indian family businesses survive the transition from first to second generation ownership. And of those that do, about half do not survive the transition from second to third generation ownership. Today's leadership paradigms have shown limited capacity to "pass it on" to future generations in their businesses.

How One Man changed the National Football League

How does discipleship work? The discipleship paradigm is designed to produce both skills and results. Through this ancient, time tested paradigm followers learn how to go beyond merely producing results for and by themselves. In order to show the extraordinary power of a discipleship paradigm consider Bill Walsh, the legendary football coach of the San Francisco 49ers. In 1979 coach Walsh inherited a 49er team that was very "ordinary" whose record the previous year was a losing 2-14. In his first year as head coach the team was still ordinary, and only won two games. The 1980 season was still pretty ordinary, but improving at 6-10. After only three short years though, the 49ers went from *ordinary to extraordinary,* winning the Super Bowl over the Cincinnati Bengals by a score of 26 to 21 in 1982. Walsh continued to exhibit extraordinary performance, winning two more Super Bowls in 1984 and 1988.

Certainly, Walsh's individual achievements were impressive. However, the full scope of Walsh's enduring impact can be seen by looking at the performance of his assistant coaches, and the coaches they coached. From

1982 to 2014, 22 Super Bowls have been played. Forty four coaches, one on each side, have been fortunate enough to play in those 22 Super Bowls. Twenty nine of the forty four coaches, or an astounding 67%, who reached the Super Bowl have been assistants to Walsh or one of his assistant coaches. In contrast to more "mercurial", loner-type head coaches, he purposely groomed or "discipled" his assistants. Consistent with the teaching a person how to teach another how to fish discipleship paradigm, Walsh taught his coaches how to coach players, but also modeled how to coach coaches. Walsh communicated this coaching philosophy in his book, Building a champion: on football and the making of the 49ers, "I coached the coaches...as the coaches taught and improved the skills of the players, the coaches were becoming more proficient themselves, and they were able to do a great job... And most of those coaches have gone on to develop their own championship teams and coaches as well. Walsh's influence on the game, through the development of his coaches, and the coach they coached is shown in the chart below.

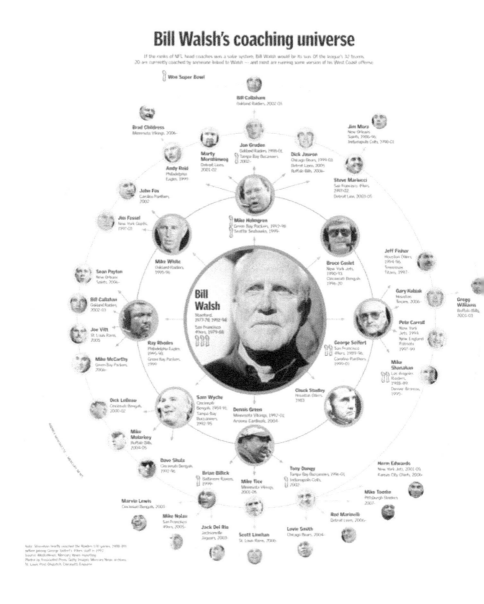

Bill Walsh's coaching universe

"When I think of Bill, that's what I think of – his Super Bowl championships, the great 49er teams that they had, and the popularization of that system *through his assistants*," said New England Patriots coach Bill Belichick. "Similar to Paul Brown, Bill had so many coaches go on to greatness – maybe all of them didn't work for Bill, but they worked and learned from someone Bill coached. That's awfully remarkable." "He was everything," star receiver Jerry Rice said. "He was the coach. He was the parent. He was the mentor. He was just like a father to me. And when I look back over my career, I know it was all about Bill Walsh."

In order to fully appreciate Walsh's achievement, let's compare his performance to that of his most successful contemporaries in terms of Super Bowl wins and appearances. Jimmy Johnson and Joe Gibbs also had three Super Bowl wins, but none of their assistant coaches achieved a Super Bowl. To illustrate the financial potential of a discipleship paradigm, let's look at the financial impact alone through a scenario where a Super Bowl victory is conservatively worth $5,000,000 in economic impact to players, coaches and the host city, and an NFC Division championship is worth $2,000,000. Using this scenario, Johnson's lifetime impact was three Super Bowls and three NFC Division titles for $21,000,000, while Walsh's total direct influence was $27,000,000. However, the total winnings of coaches who were influenced by Walsh's discipleship efforts was extraordinary. The total winnings of Walsh's assistants and their coaches listed above was a whopping thirteen super bowls and forty one NFC championships for a total of $248,000,000 *almost 10 times the impact of Johnson or Walsh alone,* as shown in the chart below. The level of influence Walsh achieved, through the number of Super Bowl winning coaches he, and his fellow coaches, produced was truly extraordinary, and changed the shape of the National Football League.

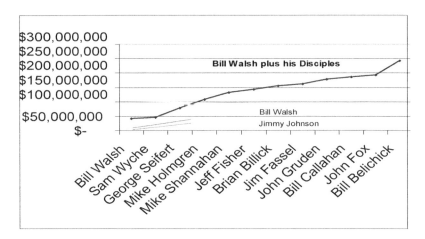

The same could be said for Andy Dorrance, Judy Foudy, and Mia Hamm who changed the state of women's soccer through the 1996 Olympic team, and millions of young women soccer players after them. Or for John Wooden, who forever changed the character of NCAA Division 1 men's basketball based upon his pyramid of values. Or for Pat Summitt, the coach of the Tennessee women's volunteers, whose consistent winning teams changed the influence and stature of women's NCAA Division 1 women's basketball. Or for Lucia Chase and Mikhail Mordkin, founders of American Ballet Theatre who "coached and discipled" multiple ballet mentors to birth a new art form of ballet in America. And many other leaders who changed their spheres of influence by investing beyond themselves. By coaching the coaches, like Walsh, through a paradigm of discipleship.

Discipleship Differs from Traditional Leadership in Several Powerful Ways

Relevant examples on the power of growing or "discipling" leaders through multiple generations can also be seen in the world of business. Often when a CEO has been brought in from the outside as a "hired gun", rather than grown from within, company performance has faltered. Consider the recent firing of outsider Jim Donald as CEO of Starbucks in 2008. Starbucks stock had declined 60% from $54 per share to $19.34. With 770 million shares of stock outstanding the $25 stock lost *$19.2 billion dollars in value*, as the chart below

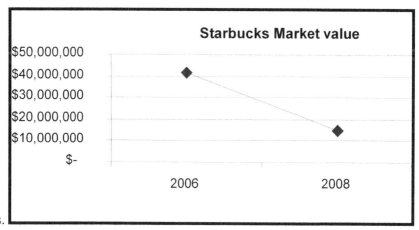

shows.

In contrast, the General Electric Company has been known for their leadership development programs and "home grown" CEOs that have been delivered good performance generation after generation. The company has bred or "discipled" a long line of CEOs which have made GE number one. From Fred Borsch in 1964 to Reginald Jones in 1973 to Jack Welch in 1981the current CEO Jeff Immelt who took the reins in 2001, G.E.'s return on equity has consistently exceeded the market, averaging 29% ROE. This remarkable run of bottom line performance can be attributed in part to G.E.'s remarkable mentoring and succession planning efforts where potential CEO candidates are identified, tested, coached, and given increasingly difficult assignments years before they are promoted to top positions.

Discipleship Results in both Skill and Performance Improvement

As a leadership researcher I was curious to explore the question of "could this ancient paradigm actually make a difference for leaders today?" In order to test the efficacy of the discipleship paradigm I conducted a study to measure the potential for improvement on skill development and organizational performance. Because I was interested in "sustainable" leadership practice, that which was not a "flash in the pan" but endured over time, I designed a longitudinal study over 18 months. For the study, business leaders in an adult professional development program were first assessed in the 7 skill areas that are explained in this book: 1) recruiting and vision casting, 2) forming a new sense of Meaningful object identity, 3) modeling and skill development, 4) skill and attitude development through probing questions and meaning-full parables, 5) strategic assignments that both teach and test, 6) constructive use of feedback through reinforcement and praise coupled with redirection, and 7) reproduction, how to teach others the skills of discipleship for influence over time.

The results of the study[3] are shown below in Figure 1 and 2 below. The students' average score before they received discipleship training was 4.49, a little better than average, on a 7 point Likert scale (7 being best). In order to see if the skill improvement would endure over time the leader's skills were measured again 18 months later after receiving the training. Their average score improved to 5.80. an astounding 28% increase! The next question was, would the leaders discipleship skills make a difference in their organizational performance? The leader's impact on organizational performance in the 8 skills averaged 4.65 before learning discipleship skills training in the program, again about average. Eighteen months later, their impact on organizational performance grew to 5.86, an increase of 26%! Next, the leaders were surveyed and asked "to what degree would you say the training affected the change in your leadership skills and performance?". On a 7 point Likert scale, the leaders responses averaged 6.2, 88% stated that their improvement was due to what they learned in the discipleship program. *Discipleship could be learned today, it improved their skills significantly, and it made a difference in their organizational performance over time.* It produced sustainable improvement, even when measured 18 months later.

Skills Improved by 28%

Performance Improved by 26%

To illustrate the potential of the discipleship paradigm over time let's compare it to a traditional leadership model. In the standard model one leader improves the performance of one person by 26% in one year. Through discipleship one leader who improves the performance of one person by 26% in one year, who then improves the performance of one other by 26% in year 2, and another in year 3, and another in year 4, and another in the fifth year. The chart below shows the difference in total impact over time:

Model	Number of People	Individual Impact	Cumulative Impact
Leadership	1	26%	26%
Discipleship			
Year 1	1	26%	26%
Year 2	2	26%	52%
Year 3	3	26%	78%
Year 4	4	26%	104%
Year 5	5	26%	130%

This is an impressive difference, 130% improvement in performance vs.26%. But what if one of the leaders was able to influence 2 persons instead of one each year, and they influenced two more, etc. Now look at what happens to the cumulative impact over time. As shown in the table and chart below the discipleship paradigm produces 130% impact with **1 person** "discipled" per year, and jumps to almost 2000% improvement in performance with only **2 people** discipled per year.

Model	Number of People	Individual Impact	Cumulative Impact
Leadership	1	26%	26%
Discipleship			
Year 1	2	26%	52%
Year 2	4	104%	156%
Year 3	8	208%	312%
Year 4	16	516%	828%
Year 5	32	1028%	1856%

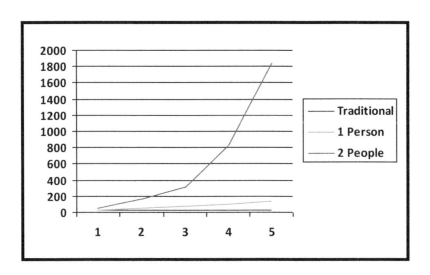

2

Observe, Test, and Reward the Right People

"In times of change, learners inherit the earth, while the learned find
themselves beautifully equipped to deal with a world that no longer exists."
Eric Hoffer

The first major task for the wise sage was to recruit the right people. He was

about to invest several years in them and utilized some simple, yet powerful methods of recruiting to qualify his leadership "investment." Pete, his first potential recruit, was a professional fisherman who had just been out fishing since midnight with his partners, and returned to shore tired and frustrated and empty-handed. His family depended on the fruit of his labors and on this day he had netted nothing- zero fish. He and his brother Andy, with their partners Jim and John in another boat, had been out fishing since the wee hours and had nothing to show for their trouble. Like an athlete who had worked out for months to compete in a big race and had finished last, Pete was very tired and exasperated. Have you ever experienced an "all-nighter" studying for an exam or prepping for a big project, presentation or client that didn't pan out? You know how that feels- you were exhausted and frustrated that you did not succeed. The last thing you wanted to do is engage in some new, demanding task. You needed and wanted to recover quickly from the ordeal. Pete, too, was ready to go home, get in bed, and sleep off the disappointment and frustration of his fruitless fishing expedition. Then something happened that would forever change Pete's life, and through him, the lives of many others.

As Pete and his friends rowed back to shore to beach their boats they were astounded by what they saw. A crowd of hundreds of people were gathered around, listening to a man giving a talk on the beach. "What were they so interested in?" they wondered. Then they recognized him. The man who drew the huge mob was a master teacher and wise leader who had quite a reputation for wisdom and knowledge. The people were pressing into each other, crowding the leader in a stressful environment of pushing and shoving to better hear him. Pete and the other fishermen had no time to listen though. They pulled their boat up onto the beach and began to wash their nets so that they could go home and sleep their frustrating night away. Pete was interrupted by the leader's voice, "Hey Pete, I'd like to get into your boat and row a few yards out into the lake. The crowd is pressing up against me and I need a bit of space!" Pete had only seconds to respond. He felt the eyes of the crowd, who revered this guy, potential customers for his fish fastening upon him. How could he say "no"? So Pete reluctantly agreed. The wise leader then got into the boat a few feet from the shore, sat down and continued to teach in earnest, thankful for a bit of space from the pushy pressure of the crowd. Pete and Andy, Jim and John busied themselves with cleaning their fishing gear and washing their nets, stewarding the tools of their trade. "Whew, am I tired. Hopefully, he'll finish his talk soon, so we can go home and get in our comfy beds" Andy whispered to Pete. "Hopefully", Pete replied.

Then Pete heard the leader's voice again directed at him personally, not the crowd. "What did He want now?" Perhaps his lecture was finished and they could go? "Pete, why don't you trying fishing out into the deep water over there?" the wise leader suggested. Pete was stunned. He was a professional fisherman and had fished all the best spots he knew. The deep water was the last place the fish would probably be because the vegetation which the fish ate was the least plentiful way out there. "Who was this guy who thinks he knows more than me? I haven't seen him out here fishing much!" Pete thought. "We just spent a half hour cleaning our gear and nets! Who does he think he is?" Pete vented his emotion, hurt, and discouragement to the leader, "Dude, we have been out there fishing the whole lake since midnight and have caught nothing!" But then thought better of it, perhaps because of the crowd of potential customers, and said, "Nevertheless, I will give it a try." So he and his partners got into their boats again and set out into the deep water. Like students who wanted to finish their homework as fast as they could so they could go outside and play, they wanted to get this "exercise" over as fast as possible.

Pete and Andy vigorously rowed out about 1 mile onto the lake. "This is deep enough," Andy thought, "let's get this over with so we can go home." Pete, being a professional fisherman, knew exactly how to place the net down into the water, gently casting it so it would barely disturb the surface and settle down to capture the unsuspecting fish. However, this was not how Pete cast his net now. Heeding Andy's words, Pete thrust the net into the water hurriedly, hoping to pull it back in and head for shore as quickly as possible. Going " through the motions" he let the net slip down a bit down in the water and then swiftly pulled on it to tug it back into the boat. Amazingly, the net tugged back! Awestruck, Pete exclaimed "it's full of fish!" "How was this possible?" Pete said with astonishment. The fish should not be here, yet here they were. In fact this was such a catch that the weight of the fish, shaking and pulsing in their nets, started to pull the boat over and cause it to sink. Pete frantically signaled to Jim and John onshore to help with the immensity of this supernatural catch. As he and his friends cruised to the shore they were astonished at the once-in-a-lifetime catch they had just landed. Pete returned to shore with a dramatically changed view of this leader. So when the wise leader asked Peter, "will you follow me and I'll teach much more than this?", Peter understandably was motivated to follow and learn from this leader.

A Leader who Care about and Serves Others

Pete was more than amazed. The wise leader was an esteemed teacher and was highly respected by the people. Usually leaders in his position bestowed their knowledge, like oracles of truth, to higher class students who were the "cream" of society in special schools. Traditional leaders of the data desired to accumulate and dispense knowledge and viewed themselves as authorities, at the "top of the food chain", and viewed others as beneath them. "What was he doing associating with me?", Pete thought. No one of his class had ever done that before. The wise leader pursued Pete because he saw something very special in him. He was drawn to Pete because he saw great potential in him, and wanted the opportunity to see Pete grow into the kind of leader who, like him, could change the world. In fact, the wise leader considered the development and growth of others like Pete to be his primary role in life. There is an old saying, "the wise elders planted trees, the fruit of which, they knew they would never live to see."

Robert Greenleaf characterized this style of leading people as "servant leadership[4]" as detailed in his essay "The leader as servant":

> The servant-leader is servant first... It begins with the natural
> feeling that one wants to serve, to serve first. Then conscious
> choice brings one to aspire to lead. That person is sharply
> different from one who is leader first, perhaps because of the
> need to assuage an unusual power drive or to acquire material
> possessions...The leader-first and the servant-first are two
> extreme types. Between them there are shadings and blends
> that are part of the infinite variety of human nature. The
> difference manifests itself in the care taken by the servant-first
> to make sure that other people's highest priority needs are
> being served. The best test, and difficult to administer, is: Do
> those served grow as persons? Do they, while being served,
> become healthier, wiser, freer, more autonomous, more likely

themselves to become servants? And, what is the effect on the least privileged in society? Will they benefit or at least not be further deprived?

Greenleaf believed that this notion of leader's acting more like servants, and less like feudal lords, is the foundation upon which a good society could be built. He said "if a better society is to be built, one that is more just and more loving, one that provides greater creative opportunity for its people, then the most open course is to raise both the capacity to serve and the very performance as servant of existing major institutions by new regenerative forces operating within them." The wise leader exemplified this notion of caring, servant leadership, and it certainly impacted Pete and his partners in big way. The leader demonstrated to Pete a level of personal care and servant hood that was very rare in his day. So it was no wonder that Pete found himself becoming open to follow him. People really don't care how much you know, until *they know how much you care*, for them.

Increasing the Odds of Recruiting the Right People

As you'll see, the wise leader's methods of discipleship were extremely powerful in changing these "ordinary" fishermen into extraordinary, world changing leaders. First of all, he hadn't haphazardly chosen Pete and his partners as his first recruits by chance. Hiring the right person in the first place can yield enormous benefits because of the savings in management time, orientation and training expenses[5] that multiply with the number of mis-hires. The cost of management time, recruiting time and job ad placements, interviewing and reference checking, loss of productivity with employee turnover, employee orientation and training, and separation costs all are factors, which can easily add up to the annual salary[6] of a lost employee. Collin's study of 1,435 companies whose stock produced results to great, chart topping performance, revealed that they do so because of the disciplined actions of their people. Disciplined actions come from disciplined thought, which in turn stems from disciplined people. Collins argues that there are several ingredients to developing *disciplined people*. He comments:

> "Effective recruiting and development of disciplined people is
> key to organizational performance. They consistently make
> better, more effective and efficient decisions- decisions that are
> informed by a unique combination of organizational mission,
> values, customer intimacy, profitability, and quality factors.
> They require little or no supervision in achieving customer
> satisfaction, quality productivity, and profitability targets.
> They are less prone to error and hence waste. How do you get
> people to share your values? You don't. You find people who
> share them and eject those who don't."

In order to change the world any leader must know how to recruit and develop a new kind of follower-- one who could perform an organization's mission, and perform well. But this leader's mission was a bit different. He wanted to produce the kind of change *that would outlive him. He wanted to create followers who could create followers who could create followers, generation after generation.* The first step was to qualify his potential recruits. At first Pete, Andy, Jim and John were not even aware they were being recruited. No resumes were submitted. No inquiries were fielded through Monster.com. The leader used the most powerful tool of recruiting in order to quality his candidates, observation. He qualified his future recruits *by observing their behavior over several weeks.* What was he looking for in his new recruits? Contrary to most job descriptions of today, he was not looking for skill. For weeks he had been observing a group of fishermen to discover what kind of basic character they possessed. For instance, how did they react when:

- They were out fishing all night, or for days, and caught nothing?
- Their nets broke and they lost some fish?
- They experienced a great catch?
- Other fishermen entered the area they were fishing in and tried to "poach" in on their catch?
- They were sick or in some way ill or injured on the job?
- One of them was late to work or missed a day?
- They were passing the time waiting for the fish to bite?
- One of them brought a particular savory lunch and would or would not share it with the others?

Recruiting by observation methods have been effectively used to assess the safety of health care practice[7], the effectiveness of occupational therapy on the performance of workers who were injured[8], in management training[9], and construction safety[10]. The Human Resource Planning Society studied the role that recruiting of global talent played in today's robust internationally competitive economy, where the skill to understand and calibrate talent is key.[11] In a recent survey 166 line managers were asked[12] to describe their own successes and failures in recruiting and hiring people. The managers attributed their success in hiring primarily to luck and intuition, and acknowledged the value of using a more *systematic and rigorous approach to recruiting and attracting personnel.*

What is the power of recruiting someone by observing their behavior when they are not aware that you are intentionally observing them as a job candidate? What you see will more likely be what you get. They will not be "play acting" or "putting on their best behavior" to impress you. They will be acting normally, just as they would if you weren't there. This wise leader was critically looking for the reactions of the fishermen in various situations and challenges they experienced over several days. Each of these situations would provide very telling examples of who they were, and clues as to what they could become.

Scouting for Talent through Observation

Professional and amateur sports coaches have known the power of observation or "scouting" for years. Anson Dorrance, head coach of the U.S. women's soccer team, saw the brand of women's soccer transform into the power it is today by scouting out Mia Hamm, Julie Foudy, Joy Fawcett, Kristine Lilly, and Brandi Chastain in 1987. Coach Dorrance stated that he knew Mia Hamm would be great, after he first observed her just one time in a practice game. Hamm showed her potential when she burst past a defensive player to score with incredible speed and tenacity. Dorrance took her raw talent, and developed her into a star. Hamm held the international record in both men and women's soccer for goal scoring at 158 for over three decades. Bill Walsh, positioned his team for the Super Bowl with only a shoe string budget by scouting out and seeing the potential of two relatively unheralded players, Joe Montana and Jerry Rice. Walsh said about Rice, who holds the NFL career pass receiving record at 1,549 catches, "I recall watching him during the season and he was a sensational player, along the lines of a John Jefferson or Wes Chandler as a receiver. He could read defenses and would fit in with our west coast style of offense." Both Dorrance and Walsh "saw" something in their future super stars, they recruited them through observation.

The Importance of Followership

After the wise leader had observed his potential recruits over time he was pretty sure that he had made the right choice for investment in training. However, he had to be positive because he was about to invest 3 years of his life in training these recruits. So he strategically designed two progressively difficult tests to assess the most important qualities in his recruits. Would they be able to follow him? Much is written and proclaimed today about leadership, but what about the art of followership? Because the wise leader wanted to teach Pete and his peers a whole new way of doing life he had to know whether Pete would be able to follow his lead.

How important is followership, the capacity to continually be open to learn and grow, in a world marked by constant change? Think about it. Who or what do we need to follow in order to be successful when the "shelf life" of what we know is increasingly shortened through worldwide change and innovation. For example, how many of you still use thermal fax paper technology, or cameras that use film from a can, or go to the Library to find data or information that you need. In times of great change how important is this skill of followership? This evidence of followership is seen in the "who rock stars" twitter feeds we follow, the "expert blogs" we follow, or the "health news and updates" we subscribe to. Developing skill in followership of societal trends, innovation, customer needs and wants, changes in the people we know and love, and the larger movements in our world in essential for survival and success in any pursuit. Thus, how people were recruited to test their ability to follow to the ancient paradigm of discipleship becomes even more relevant today, doesn't it?

This is a Test of Followership, it is only a Test

The efficacy of pre-employment screening or testing to determine the feasibility or fit of individuals for a job has been well documented. Physical, task or psychological tests have been found to provide greater degrees of confidence in the hiring process. A key difference between these tests and more common pre-employment screening exams was the focus on emotional recovery and life-long learning. The wise leader was not interested in assessing how much Pete knew, as much as his openness to learning and new ways of doing things. People who are not open to change and learning, like the dinosaurs of old, will find themselves exquisitely prepared for a world that no longer exists. According to Drucker[13] (1997), in order to succeed in a challenging economic environment one must harness "the intelligence and spirit of people at all levels of an organization to continually build and share knowledge". The leader designed two tests to increase significantly in level of challenge to "follow" him into new ways of learning as follows:

1. The First Followership Test- Lower Degree of Challenge

First, the wise leader designed an initial test with a lower degree of challenge to qualify his potential recruits in their "followership" ability. The fishermen he targeted to recruit had not had a great night, they had returned to shore with nothing. Zero fish. The wise leader then asked the eldest of the fishermen, Pete, "can I use your boat for a while to deliver a lecture?" This test was challenging because Pete, and the fishermen had been out all night and wanted to go home, eat, and sleep. Thus, the first test was designed to see if Pete would be open to new learning from this leader, even when what he was asking challenged his existing experience and knowledge. Why is this so important? Because the leader was about to lead Pete and the other fishermen recruits in an entirely new and unknown skill set, so the ability to trust and follow the leader into the unknown was essential. These "follow the leader" type tests in recruiting may be even more important in today's economy, which is marked by times of rapid and constant change. The shelf life of knowledge today in most fields can be as little as three months. For example, in health care, even the most experienced surgeons attend training workshops about every 6 months or they will be passed up by others who know more than they do. The wise leader was about to invest 3 years of his life in Pete and his friends. He had to know that Pete would be open to learning and following him. Otherwise, why bother?! The wise leader had to know the answer that no employment survey question could tell him. Would Pete follow him, no matter what he asked him to do? -whether Pete emotionally "felt" like it or not. Pete passed the first test.

2. Second Followership Test- High Degree of Challenge

After this, an even more challenging exercise was designed to again test, and reward Pete's decision to follow the wise leader. In it, the wise leader called Pete, professional fishermen, to sail his boat out into deep water to fish. Thus, Pete's "professional" knowledge and ability to learn in an area of "expertise" was tested. Pete and his fishing partners had invested their entire evening fishing but had caught nothing- nada-zip. Now, this man was giving them advice on fishing? Pete was probably thinking, "I've already fished out there, and caught nothing! What are you thinking!#?" What the wise leader wanted to know was this- would Pete be open to learn and follow the leader in an area that he assumed he knew better? Secondly, this test first presented an emotional and leadership challenge. Pete wanted to go home, eat and sleep off the frustrating emotions of coming home empty handed! How would he respond? Would Pete be able to recover emotionally from his fishing failure and follow the leader? Would the others follow his lead? This discipleship recruiting through observation followed by two "open to learn and grow" tests is diagrammed below.

 Recruiting through Observation >

 Followership initial challenge Test 1 >

 Followership Bigger Challenge Test 2

The Promise of Earned Rewards- What's In it for Me?

Fortunately for Pete, he decided to follow the wise leader's directions. Pete's choice to follow was strongly rewarded with a great catch of fish. The wise leader did not ask Pete to "blindly follow" him, but provided Pete the opportunity to earn a sound reward for doing so. Hence, Pete was given two tests, of increasing difficulty, that would enable the wise sage to determine his ability to follow. Leadership and followership is a two way street. These two recruiting tests gave the wise leader a chance to see if Pete would follow him, as well as an opportunity to prove himself to Pete. A fundamental question that all workers ask themselves when applying for any job is *"what's in it for me?"* Pete "passed" the tests, the wise leader was able to earn Pete's trust through caring, servant leadership, and Pete was rewarded for doing so. The promise of a significant, surprise reward strongly influenced Pete's response to follow the wise leader[14].

Why is the promise of earning a reward so powerful in recruiting? Rewards that reinforce the right choices and learning have been shown to be powerful motivators of behavior. As humans, we are motivated to meet our basic needs for survival, including behavioral drives for food, water, sex, warmth and shelter, attachment and affection[15]. Experiments on rats in the 1950s showed that rats, whose brains are like humans, regulate their behavior based upon the promise of rewards that they can earn. Olds and Milner 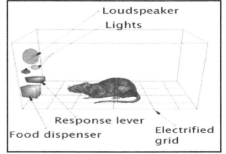 (1954)[16] discovered that low-voltage electrical stimulation of various regions in rat's brains activated "reward and pleasure system" areas. He used these reward systems to teach the animals to run mazes and solve problems more effectively, using a Skinner box as shown above. They experimented with electrical stimulation in humans and found that humans reacted with sensations of pleasure and reward as well.

Reward Based Behavior

Rewards that strongly influenced behavior were those that were necessary for the survival of species, such as food, significant relationships, or successful aggression. Secondary rewards, or those that were found to be less important, derive their value from primary rewards. In 1985, Dr. Benjamin Bloom conducted a study to understand how people develop from novices to world-class talent. He interviewed 120 people who had achieved world-class success as concert pianists, sculptors, tennis champions, Olympic swimmers, research neurologists, and mathematicians. Bloom also noted that individually customized rewards, like fish for fishermen, were important in the development of these world class performers. Here is an excerpt from an interview with a world class pianist on the power of rewards:

> There was an awful lot of praise and an awful lot of attention.
> Play for the family, play for this one, play for that one. There
> was so much reward for performing that I've always loved it,
> the opportunity to play in a recital, or travel to "the big city" to
> perform as part of a more renowned orchestra. What kept a six
> year old at a piano for an hour a day practice was different
> from what would reward 2 to 3 hours a day of practice when
> the child reached 13 years of age.

Recruit for Mission and Values, Train for Skill

Today the mantra in many companies is to recruit for values[17], train for skill. How long does it take to grow values or character in a person? Most parents would say anywhere from 18 to 45 years! Today, more than ever, it makes sense to recruit potential employees with ones values in mind in order to invest training in the right people. A company's values may contribute significantly to its reputation in the marketplace and may create goodwill and positive image in the minds of prospective recruits.[18] At General Electric, every hire must have a good fit with G.E.'s core values of lean, agile, creative, collective sense of ownership, and reward. It is essential to know and use methods that enable you to observe, recruit, and reward of the right people, with the right fit for you and your organization.

How do you find people that are good candidates or a good "fit" ?

Alright then, how do you actually pull this kind of recruiting through observation, tests, followership and promise of reward. Apprenticeships or internships may provide a good source from which to observe and qualify potential employees for a good fit for company values. They are a low cost method (interns may often work for free or low cost in return for gaining work experience) of providing observational opportunities for future recruits. Leading organizations and universities such as Starbucks, General Electric, Boeing, Columbia University, Mead, University of Indiana, and Ford have found internships to be a valuable source of new employees. Like baseball coaches do in AA and AAA "farm" teams, organizations use their internships to try out and discover motivated, gifted people before hiring. If the intern makes the cut, the company may make him or her a job offer. Service learning internships from local colleges or short term internship hires may also provide opportunities where specific values or skills may be observed to see how the intern performs in X circumstance or situation. For example, if a company values initiative, an intern might be assigned several tasks where the ability to take initiative with a fellow employee, customer, or stakeholder was essential for success. The intern may gain valuable benefits as well including hands-on work experience, marketable skills and marketplace network contacts. Certainly, probationary employments or assignments provide a similar opportunity to place prospective "intern observees" in selected tasks in order to see how they fare. "Internships are the ideal interview tool," said Jillian Donnelly, president of CareerExposure.com. Internships let employers have the opportunity to evaluate potential new hires and determine whether the candidate is a good fit for the company. Z University.org recently completed a five-year study that demonstrated that employers benefited from college interns and realized substantial gains in productivity even without hosting students on site. General Electric tests future leaders and managers through its Crotonville executive training site. In large classroom settings, senior G.E. leaders present real world problems (increasing market share in China) to managers to observe and test the thinking and reasoning abilities of upcoming manager "recruits".

What are some other ways to observe potential new recruits in action?

- at other stores or organizations in your community

- in non profit or volunteer work settings

- in assignments with local colleges where new recruits may surface and be tested

How Southwest Airlines recruits Value-Able People

Southwest Airlines recruiters do not look for a fixed set of skills when recruiting. They are searching for something far more important – *the kind of values* that will set Southwest apart. The recruiters are seeking value-able people, with the kind of energy, humor, team spirit, and self-confidence which matches Southwest's distinctive customer-service culture.[19] Southwest looks for people whose devotion to customer and company amounts to a sense of personal mission and passion. What techniques do Southwest recruiters use to find the elite few that meet their culture and values?

Southwest uses a combination of scenarios and role plays where people's attitudes, behavior and core values may be observed. In one scenario, potential recruits fill out and read aloud a personal "Coat of Arms" - a questionnaire on which applicants complete statements such as, "One time when my sense of humor helped me was_____"; "A time I reached my peak performance was _____"; "My personal motto is _____." Most of the answers are unremarkable. But all of them give strong clues about a person's deeper values and convictions- people with the kind of passion Southwest is seeking to discover. Another value testing exercise is called Fallout Shelter. Applicants are told to imagine that they are to be the developers of a committee that will rebuild the nation after a just-declared nuclear war. They are then asked to choose 7 people out of 15 people from different occupations: nurse, teacher, all-star athlete, politician, biochemist, pop singer. They then are given 10 minutes to make a unanimous decision about which seven people can remain in a bomb shelter and life. The job contestants go through a "storming" stage of group dynamics where they argue, influence, discuss, defend, offend, and deliberate on various solutions. Interviewers then watch the group observe and rate people's values of leadership, service, assertiveness, and confidence that are important for Southwest.

Recruiting Exercise

Here is a step by step exercise you can use for your recruiting efforts:

1. Determine what venues exist where you can observe the potential of the new recruit (i.e., create internships, visit their existing workplace as a secret customer, engage with them at business networking events such as Rotary or chamber meetings, or in volunteer organizations).

2. Once you have identified a potential candidate, design some suitable low and higher degree challenge tests that will help you determine what your new candidate is "made of".

a. Low degree of challenge test:

_____

_____

b. Higher degree of challenge

test:_____

_____

3. Determine how to contextualize your mission to communicate it in terms of the candidates interests and motivations (i.e., if you were recruiting for G.E. you'd think about the agile and high energy values of your company mission).

_____

_____

4. Design a reward system that offers the promise of rewards or compensations that recruits can earn by coming to work with you.

_____

_____

3

Meaningful Object Identity

"So I'm ugly. I never saw anyone hit with his face." Yogi Berra

The next step the wise leader would normally include training his new recruits how to do the job. But as we'll see he included a non intuitive, yet essential step *before starting the investment in training.* We rejoin Pete and the fishermen... What Pete heard the wise leader say made little sense to him, at first.

> "You are the salt of the earth. But if the salt loses its saltiness, how can it be made salty again? It is no longer good for anything, except to be thrown out and trampled by men. You are the light of the world. A city on a hill cannot be hidden. Neither do people light a lamp and put it under a bowl. Instead they put it on its stand, and it gives light to everyone in the house."

Pete thought to himself, "Why is this leader saying that I'm salt? I don't get it." The wise leader formed an identity in his followers as those who helped to clean up a tainted world by living good lives and setting an example for others. Although Pete didn't realize it at first, the wise leader was redefining his identity *through meaningful objects that were significant to them*, salt and light. If there was anything that was meaningful to a fisherman in Pete's day, it would be the value of salt. Unlike today, where salt is plentiful and inexpensive (about $5 dollars for 10 pounds today) salt was a very precious commodity in the Roman Empire. Roman soldiers were paid an allowance of salt called a salarium. The word salary is derived from salt. In that day 10 pounds of salt was worth about one month of the average workers' wages! The Roman military, fortified with salt, could fight longer and stronger than most opponents. Wars were fought, economies made or broken and slaves were even traded for salt. The estimated worth of slaves in trade for salt is said to have given rise to the common expression "he is not worth his salt."

Salt was an element that was used in ancient times as a disinfectant, preservative, seasoning, unit of commerce, and as a tonic for physical health. Salt water had been used to disinfect infected body parts, just as a sore throat may be helped by gargling with salt water. The fishermen were very familiar with what happened to meat that was not cured in salt, it would rot, draw flies, and create a stench of bacteria and disease. To Pete light represented an important source of value also. In ancient times when there was no light from a candle or oil lamp people's lives were greatly affected, all productive work would have to stop. If Pete understood that if he didn't have enough money to purchase oil, and have light, his productivity and livelihood could be significantly affected. The wise leader changed their view of themselves using a method I call *meaningful object identity*, with objects that were full of meaning and significance for the fishermen, salt and light.

Transformation through Meaningful Object Identity- from "Stinky" to High Value

Why did Pete need a change in his core identity? In his day there were two classes of people-- the higher ruling or governing class, and the lower worker or vocational class. Pete was doing his best to survive on the lower rung of society. Most of the time he avoided contact with people of the other class because they "turned up their nose at him!" Why? Because most of the time he "stunk". He smelled fishy. When you worked with fish all day, the fish oil and smell permeated your clothes, body, equipment, everything. Pete didn't appreciate people looking at him funny and commenting about his fishy stench. He may have felt "worth less" because he was looked down upon by many. Understandably, he didn't want to associate with them very much, and spent his time in the company of other fishermen, who wouldn't put him down. This may be why fishermen's communities like the Boston crab and Alaskan tuna communities exist, even today.   However, this presented a problem for the wise leader. His mission for Pete and the others involved reaching people, even people who Pete didn't want to associate with. Thus, the leader had to find a way to redefine Pete's sense of identity, his self-esteem in order to have any chance of his mission being accomplished. Otherwise, his mission was doomed to failure!

Therefore, the wise leader purposefully defined their identity by associating key character attributes with elements that were meaningful in the fishermen's lives. He transformed their identity from that of being "the scum of the earth" to salt and light- some of the most valuable elements on earth to them as shown in the Figure below. By creating a remarkable new self of identity and esteem, in salt and light, the most valuable elements of the day, the wise leader radically changed the fisherman's self esteem. This new identity was designed to enable them to see their great sense of worth, even when the public did not, at least at first.

"Stinky, I'm Worth-less"

Current Identity   **Mission**

"I'm very valuable, like Salt & Light"

Transformed Identity   **Mission**

Mission Statements are Not Enough

Many leadership drills today involve getting people to "buy in" to a new mission or vision statement. However, it appears that the mission or vision statement may represent only part of the leadership equation. Another key task for leaders is answering the question of "how can I change my people's hearts and minds, their core identity and beliefs, to adopt the new mission?"

Here's a case in point. A few weeks ago I stopped into a local auto repair franchise for an oil change. Their mission statement was proudly posted on the wall, and read something like "precision craftsmen creating great performance..." What I heard while sitting down in the waiting room was not consistent with this mission- it was the sound of an air gun rattling on and on and on, in a frustrated attempt to either take off, or put on, a tire! This shoddy worker's actions were nothing like the "precision craftsmen" alluded to in the proudly posted mission statement. I'm sure you've had a similar experience at another retail store like "the customer is always right" or "world class customer service", where their work did not match the aspirations of their posted store motto or mission statement. The mission statement at this auto shop was like a freeway exit sign that people drove right by, and was no guarantee of performance. Thus, the strategic choice of an object that vividly represents the new identity that your people must adopt in order to fulfill their mission is crucial.

Meaningful Object Identity seems to be more foundational to a person's core being than what their mission is or what they do. A new sense of identity answers the question of "who am I?", and what gives meaning and purpose to my life. One's sense of identity provides the foundation for meaning and purpose, and future mission. For example, think of the way Spock in the Star Trek series wrestled with his half human mother, half Vulcan father in a logic vs. emotional tug of war. Because, like the fishermen, he was experiencing strong pressure from his logical, Vulcan culture he thought he too should adopt an identity devoid of emotion and subject to logic only.

But only when he, through the example and dialogue of a mentor in Captain Kirk and others, he realized that he could be strongly logical and also emotional, and adopted an "best of both worlds" identity. Once his core identity was reconciled within himself, Spock was able to attain to a strong sense of mission and service to the people's of the universe. Identity was foundational for Spock realization of his mission "to go where no one had gone before into strange new worlds." What I'm trying to suggest is that identity is foundational to mission. If someone, like the fisherman or Spock, is unclear or wrestling with their sense of identity, their ability to achieve any mission can be compromised. Thus, we view Meaningful Object Identity as an essential foundation for building a new mission or mission statement upon, as shown in the Figure below.

Mission

Meaningful Object Identity

A Meaningful Object Identity of salt and light, for example, like a multi-faceted diamond provided great sense of personal meaning and worth as well as powerful benefits and impact to the society of the day. To the fishermen, salt and light was personally meaningful, and changed their worth-less identity into that of the most valuable elements on earth. Secondly, the instrumental value of salt and light to benefit society was also clear, both were highly valued elements that were essential to support life in their day. How you view yourself really does matter. If my identity and view of myself is "worth-less", chances are, I will act and behave accordingly. My life may have a lesser impact on people because I really don't see myself as being able to contribute

 anything of great value to society. Wise leaders will utilize the power Meaningful Object Identity because it has the capacity to change someone's self esteem and image. Like the feline in the mirror below who sees himself as a lion. Chances are, with a "lion-like" identity he will view himself as one who can act with courage and power in taking on big challenges in life.

The Powerful Influence of Identity in Sports

The power of a sense of identity can be seen in the realm of sports, bringing a sense of unity and purpose to people's, and even nation's lives. In the 1970s, the Pittsburgh Steelers defense was characterized by the front four players on the defensive line who were known as the "steel curtain" that made running the ball against them almost impossible. Likewise, the San Francisco 49ers dynasty of the 1980s was identified by their creative "west coast" offense which was characterized by and identified with short, high percentage passes. Brazil, and hence Brazilians, identify with their prowess at the game of soccer and hence expect to do well at World Cup soccer matches. Russians identify themselves with strength in gymnastics and expect to perform well at the Olympics as a source of national identity. In Seattle, football fans fly a "12 man" flag signifying their identity as rooters and supporters of the team.

The "Twelves", who view themselves as twelfth person additional members of the 11 man offense or defense have actually affected the outcomes of games. The 12s yell so loudly, that opposing offensive or defensive team members cannot hear the plays being called by the quarterback or coaches during a game correctly. As a result the other team is forced to make mistakes, gets offside penalties, or misinterprets plays. Could the behavior of the 12th man have actually helped the Seahawks win enough games to get in the Super Bowl? If you were to ask a 12, he or she would probably say "yes"! The people of a city or nation may identify with these sports and are provided a sense of national identity which powerfully spans class, race and distance.

Why Identity is so Powerful

Why do we have such a need to identify with a certain group- to be a "12th person" football fan, mimic a superhero, or get a "must have" Iphone, as shown in the symbols above? These images, as *objects that are meaningful or significant* to the people who are associated with and purchase them, are powerful sources of identity for them. Identity theory[20] explains this powerful phenomenon. A social identity is a person's knowledge that he or she belongs to a social category or group, like being a sports fan. People are motivated to behave in ways that maintain and boost their sense of self-esteem or significance, in connection with others who feel the same way. When a person's self-esteem is higher they may perceive themselves as more attractive, competent, likable or good.

However, when self-esteem and the positive aspects that it may provide are lacking, a person may feel more alone and disconnected which may create feelings of anxiety and isolation. A person may associate themselves with a team identity by wearing the teams colors, singing the team fight song and knowing the players' names and statistics. They connect and identify with the team as if they themselves were playing the game.

The 1936 eight man Olympic gold medal rowing team discovered the power of having a shared identity in Berlin. Over 70 years later, a member of that team was still able to recall the significance of a having a shared sense of identity:

> They were now representatives of something much larger than themselves - a way of life, a shared set of values. Liberty was perhaps the most fundamental of those values. But the things that held them together - trust in each other, mutual respect, humility, fair play, watching out for one another... a shared experience—a singular thing that had unfolded in a golden sliver of time long gone, when nine good-hearted young men strove together, pulled together as one, gave everything they had for one another, bound together forever by pride and respect and love. Joe was crying, at least in part, for the loss of that vanished moment but much more, I think, for the sheer beauty of it.[21]

How does identity translate into performance? Harvard professors Leonard and Swap[22] explored the question of how business wisdom or "deep smarts" is learned in organizations. They looked at how dot.com CEOs learned and taught key skills including managing the board, developing venture capital, managing people and scaling the company in the troubling years of the dot.bomb era. Leonard and Swap found that people's deep belief systems or identities significantly influence how they built, transferred and reacted to new knowledge. Successful entrepreneurs were aware of their deep beliefs or identity, and this affected their decisions and actions. For example, those with a personal identity of "doing well by doing good" founded companies that were economically viable *and benefited society.* One of the CEOs founded Care2, an electronic greeting card company that gave 10% of its profits to environment enhancing nonprofits.

Bloom, in his study of what ingredients combined to develop world class athletes, musicians and scientists found that all of them shared a sense of identity with their craft. Here is a quote for a world renowned pianist on her special identity with the piano:

> I became identified with the piano. That was the only way I
> could stand out and be someone special. Even though I
> resisted it, it was part of my identity from when I was very
> young.

A core sense of identity can affect performance. Shih and company[23] tested how people's sense of identity affected their performance on a challenging mathematics test. They were given an opportunity to agree or disagree with a statement that referenced a gender or ethnic strength or weakness. When females identified with the statement that "women do poorly at math" their performance suffered. While Asian women who identified with the statement "Asians do better at math" performed better in the test. Thus, one's identity is a significant influence in how they view life and perform. McInnes[24] looked at the how employees view their identity affected their behavior in times of organizational change in health care organizations. The research revealed that when the formation of worker's identities was left to chance without any communication or leadership, workers views of their identities and those of others *caused a great deal of conflict, and worked against progress or change.*

However, when the formation of people's identities was intentionally facilitated by leadership, *barriers to change were lessened*. The study suggested that leaders need to facilitate the process of people forming their identities, and how they perceive the identities of others:

• An active effort needs to be made by leadership to facilitate discussion of how people view their identity, and the identities of others. It was helpful to facilitate discussion about the questions people may have about their identity within the organization. Questions of "Who am I and who are you within the context of our group or organization? What is my role, and your role?" may need to be addressed.

•   An interactive cycle is recommended where a degree of agreement on "who we are" and "what our roles are" is defined, and then revisited over time for continued clarification.

One of the best examples of how leaders can utilize a sense of identity to contribute to great performance can be learned from John Wooden. Wooden, who led his UCLA basketball teams to 10 national championships between 1963 and 1975, is probably the greatest coach in NCAA Division One collegiate basketball history. What reason does Wooden give to explain his amazing success? Like "salt and light" Wooden detailed a distinctive identity in a "Pyramid of Success" that enabled his players to achieve enduring greatness. The pyramid is comprised of 25 distinctive values that build upon one another and culminated in competitive greatness. Wooden talks about the importance of one of the core values that formed a new identity for his players, industriousness, this way:

"Tiger Woods? Peyton Manning? Anyone else you might care
to mention who has achieved personal success and competitive
greatness has a strong sense of identity– Michael Jordan's love
of the game, Jack Nicklaus relentless pursuit of perfection,
Oprah Winfrey's connection with people, Sam Walton's love of

people and customers, and the list goes on. Businessperson, clergy, doctor, lawyer, plumber, artist, writer, coach, or athlete, all share a fundamental sense of identity that helps them to achieve competitive greatness."[25]

Pat Summitt, Head Coach of the Tennessee Lady Volunteers has won eight national championships, more than any other ladies coach in NCAA history. Here's what she said about the importance of identity in recruiting for her championship teams . "First I want to get to know the players in the recruiting process. I want to know if they are the right fit for Tennessee. Are they highly motivated? Are they goal oriented? Are they unselfish? Do they have a good work ethic? Are they competitive?" Summit stated, "I want to know what their values are. This has really given us an edge. Knowing your players well can help you to give them an emotional edge. You can dial them up. And I think that, in a close game, that's more important than the execution on the offensive or defensive end. There are times when you need an emotional edge. And when you can get that emotional edge you can succeed." Identity appears to provide a core sense of "who am I?" and acts as a strong foundation for future skill development and extraordinary performance as shown below.

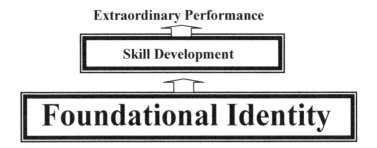

Extraordinary Performance

Skill Development

Foundational Identity

A Real Life Success Story of Meaningful Object Identity

Let me relate an actual story from one of the leaders in the executive education program, who we'll call Josie. Each leader's assignment, like the wise leader's example of salt and light, was to change a troubling situation at work, home or life by crafting a new Meaningful object identity for a person or group. Josie's situation was that she and her husband were both working hard to better their lives and save money to purchase a home. For Josie, however, a level of intimacy and celebration between she and her husband was lacking because they were both just so busy. Josie wanted to create an opportunity for her and her husband to pause and reflect on what was happening in their lives, and to celebrate all that they were experiencing, to appreciate their hard work. So Josie thought "what is the meaningful or significant object? What can I choose that could communicate this new identity of pausing in a meaningful way to my husband?" Then it came to her; the T.V remote control! The remote had a "pause" button on it. Could this work? Would her husband relate to this pause button as an opportunity to take a moment with her to reflect and celebrate life in the midst of their busy schedules? She was a little concerned about how her husband would react. Sometimes he would come home after work so tired that he had little margin left for conversation.

Josie decided it was worth a try and invited her husband to a special dinner to talk about it with him on a Saturday night. Saturday morning was their sleep in day and they would be in a good place emotionally, and would have recovered from the work week. After dinner Josie said to her husband, "we're both working really hard and saving a ton of money toward getting our dream house, which is so cool." "Yes, isn't it?!" her husband, who we'll call Rick said. "However, I want to talk about something else that is really important to me, as important as the dream house." "Okay..." Rick replied. Josie walked over and picked up the remote from the coffee table and brought it over to the dinner table. "Sweetheart, I feel like our lives are just so busy and that we come home so focused on our work, or so tired, that we never get any time for each other. It's like our lives are constantly on "fast forward" (pushing the button on the remote). I feel like we're going so fast and pushing so hard that we're missing our chances to reflect and celebrate about what we've accomplished! I was hoping that we could do something differently, that we could press the "pause" button once in a while and take a break to talk about what's happening in our lives, be grateful, and enjoy our successes."

To Josie's amazement, Rick responded, "Wow! I really see what you mean. I mean, I get it with the remote- pressing the pause button for a sec to reflect on what is going on with us and to celebrate 'us' a bit more. The remote has other buttons you know..." What Rick said next really blew Josie's mind. "What if each one of us could say to the other 'stop'- like pressing the stop button? Or 'rewind' if we say or do something that we did in the heat of the moment and would like to take back- something that, in retrospect, we regret?!" Stunned (what was happening between Rick and her was beyond her wildest dreams), Josie said, "well, uh, yes, I guess this would be okay too. In fact (with a sense of hope and joy) I think I'd like to stop or rewind sometimes too!" Because the remote was a *meaningful object that her husband Rick could relate to* he responded in a way that surpassed Josie's greatest hopes.

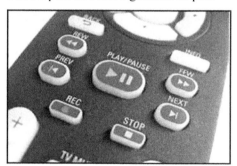

Here are some examples of Meaningful Objects and the new Identity they reflect in various organizational settings:

- Booster seat- IT customer service, helps people out of their "hole" and up to the table, understand how to use the system (utensils) so they can eat/enjoy their meal (OS, Excel).

- Thermostat- a change agent, instead of a thermometer that regulates the temperature or status of something, the thermostat has the temperature or status.

- Window v. mirror- leadership humility that looks out the window to give recognition and in the mirror to apportion blame or fault.

Steps to forming a new sense of identity for people you influence

Here are some practical steps to form a new sense of identity for your people:

1. What is the condition of the hearts and minds of your people, their current identity (i.e., fishermen were outcasts, lived apart from the mainstream of society, and kept to themselves)?

_____

_____

2. What is your vision for your people? (i.e., fishermen- engage the culture, reach the world)

_____

_____

3. What fundamentally needs to change in your people's hearts and minds in order to accomplish the vision, what new identity (i.e., fishermen's identity needed to change from "worthless" to people of great value and intrinsic worth in society) needs to be formed?

_____

_____

4. What object (i.e., salt and light were greatly prized and valued by society) will be Meaningful to your people to form this new identity?

_____

_____

4

Show and Tell: The Power of Domain Immersion Modeling

"You can observe a lot just by watching." Yogi Berra

Once the identity of the fishermen was transformed the wise sage turned to the subject of training to succeed at their new domain of health care. In Pete's day the traditional teachers and leaders, like many University lecturers today, typically invited their new recruits into the classroom and instructed them on the finer points of their marketplaces and organizations. Leaders today attempt to lead through various forms of "throwing their voice around" as well. We tell, we lecture, we plead, we rant, we raise our voice for emphasis, we inflect, like coaches on the sidelines with large megaphones-- with little effect. As Pete soon discovered, the wise leader "taught" very differently. He defined the key skills that he wanted his people to excel in and then *showed and modeled* what greatness looked like-- how to teach, sell and do health care with new customers. The wise leader utilized the most powerful lesson for how people learn, domain immersion modeling. What is domain immersion modeling and why is it so powerful? Because "Show and Tell" is much greater than tell alone.

Show and Tell > Tell

Medical domain immersion modeling - See one, do one, teach one

From the early 19th century on, most medical education in the United States was administered through an internship system where students were "immersed" in their new domain. The interns received hands-on instruction from a local practitioner and/or through clinical training at a hospital using what is called "see one, do one, teach one" methodology. Like a piece of white cloth that was dunked in India ink to change its properties, the new intern was completely engrossed in the everyday practice of medicine at the hospital. Through this immersion, he or she experienced, on an emotional, logical and practical level, dramatic emergency room visits, sore throat diagnoses, the trauma of surgery, and normal everyday rounds. A medical intern was "apprenticed" to more experienced doctors and learned to practice medicine under their mentorship.

How does domain immersion modeling work in health care, for example? In a medical model, the intern first learns to perform a task, say, heart surgery, by **observing** an expert resident, which was referred to as "see one." The intern watches lots of surgeries until they develop the confidence and competence to perform one on their own, which was referred to as "do one." Eventually the intern is allowed to practice and perform the surgery herself under close supervision of a resident physician. After they have done enough of them successfully, confidently and competently, they join a physician's network, become a medical doctor and open up their own practices. They become certified to "teach one."

See one   **Do one**   **Teach One**

But what about people who worked a certain way for a long time? Can you teach an "old dog new tricks" in a new domain?   A recent study by William Branch, M.D.[26] showed that effort does matter, and showed that even established clinicians can learn to adopt new skills in new domains of health care, and can become better teachers and role models in the process. Groups of veteran physician-teachers from five different academic medical centers met at least twice a month to practice skills designed to enhance compassion, or reflect on their own work through discussion and narrative writing. After 18 months residents and medical students evaluated their physician-teachers, versus a control group of doctors, on issues of compassion including listening carefully, teaching communication and relationship-building skills, and inspiring the adoption of caring attitudes toward patients- just like the servant leadership model of the wise leader. In each of the five centers, those physician-teachers who participated in the program consistently outscored the control group doctors. Dr. Branch stated his surprise at the results, "We all know there are huge problems in health care now. So many doctors are pushed to feel they can only spend so much time with patients. They lacked the kind of skills that we now know can be taught and modeled, so their brief encounters aren't satisfying for either the doctors or the patients." Branch's study reinforced the modeling methods of the wise leader.

Modeling for Character

Modeling appears to offer promise for the formation of moral values and character as well. A recent random survey of people at all organizational levels by the Ethics Research Center[27] showed that ethical concerns are higher than they were in 1994, the date of the ERC's previous study. The study showed that key ethics outcomes were more positive when employees saw ethical values like honesty, respect, and trust applied frequently at work. And perhaps more importantly, when "organizational leaders and supervisors are seen as modeling ethical behavior." Modeling of ethical behavior by organizational leaders, supervisors, and coworkers increased employees overall satisfaction with their organization and reduced turnover. Just like the ethical servant leadership style which the wise leader modeled, caring about and for the person, significantly impacting the character development of the fishermen.

Mirror Neurons explain the Power of Modeling

Recent research on leadership behavior has revealed leaders preference for one on one meetings to "coach" and "guide" staff in training. Typically this has involved the leader lecturing or telling a staff member how to do a certain job. However, new findings from brain research laboratories, based on studies of subjects ranging from monkeys to police officers, are offering fresh insights into how human beings learn and how leaders can best deliver their instruction to achieve better results[28]. The research has focused on clusters of specialized cells in an area  of the brain involved in planning movements. A new kind of cell, *called a mirror neuron,* was discovered.

The surprising power of these special cells surfaced by accident in a research laboratory in Italy where scientists were studying how the brain cells of macaque monkeys worked in response to movement. In their experiments, when a monkey grabbed a peanut certain cells on either side of its brain "fired" (activated) as measured by a brain scanner. Then one day a monkey which was hooked up to the scanner for an experiment just happened to see a hungry lab assistant grab a peanut to eat. The same neurons fired in the monkey's brain. The brain's cells were activated in the same way when the monkey was actually doing something and when it was *merely seeing something being done*. The same neurons in the monkey's brain fired. The brain seemed to "mirror" the activity the monkey was seeing. This research emphasizes the importance and power of modeling behavior in training. It appears that the "show and tell" techniques we learned in kindergarten are still very powerful today.

According to Jim Krug[29], consultant with the Development Institute of Denver Colorado, "… approximately 75% of leadership development occurs on the job". Modeling leadership behaviors on the job are a powerful way to teach. Dr. Bill Lewinski[30], executive director of the Police Science Research Center at Minnesota State University, states that what's being discovered about mirror neurons suggests "profound implications about how police officers need to be trained. The more an instructor can stimulate mirror neurons through modeling, the greater the chance that officers can readily pick up new skills. Also they will clue in more quickly to recognizing when those skills need to be used for their own protection."

When a police recruit sees how an instructor manipulates a pistol to fire accurately or performs complex targeting moves, their own ability to reproduce these skills improves. Police Science National Board Member Gary Klugiewicz, an experienced police trainer emphasized the power of modeling on behavior even through a bad example. He recalled an embarrassing moment as a martial arts trainer when his students were demonstrating drills for another master. The master watched for a while, then commented: "These must be your students because they are all doing the same thing wrong that you are. If you are modeling incorrectly," Klugiewicz said, "your students will learn to perform incorrectly and not even know it." Contact and modeling by an adept leader appears to be most important as new recruits enter an organization.

Whenever possible, real life examples and modeling is preferred over role play scenarios. Training programs that use theory to train leaders instead of practice have been found to be less than effective. How can staff be expected to deal with real life situations if the right behavior in those situations is not modeled for them? Individuals need to know how to deal with situations in the workplace and they cannot learn these skills in lecture-based academic settings. Organizations are attempting to build these realistic training scenarios into their programs by having exemplary leaders give demonstrations or lead discussion in developing these "soft skills"[31] Modeling provides trainees with examples of real world problems and real world solutions.

Lewinski comments on the power of modeling over teaching by lecture. In academies and in-service training, instructors often teach by lecture because it's easier, but just talking about something or reading about it is not enough. We need to be repeatedly incorporating actual physical examples that officers can watch when we are trying to teach skills that can be modeled. Role playing how a suspect might act is not sufficient, unless the role-player is a very highly skilled actor. Your students need to see real suspects in real situations, because their facial expressions, voice tone, language, and overall behavior will be genuine. This will help officers in the class begin to notice and absorb subtle cues of deception, for example. Then when they see such cues again--on the street--there will be recognition, set off by their mirror neurons firing like crazy, that will make the hair on the back of their neck stand up as a warning sign.

Modeling Exercise

Here is an exercise to develop your skills in modeling. Think about the people you desire to lead or influence right now and ask yourself the following questions:

1. How much of the time when I'm trying to get someone to do something the "right" way do I invest telling or lecturing them? How much of the time do I spend modeling or showing them how to do something?

_____

_____

2. What are some ways, projects or circumstances in which I can model behavior for the people I work with?

_____

_____

_____

3. In what areas can I add an element of "showing" to my "telling" people what to do?

_____

_____

_____

5

Powerful Tools to Change the Way People Think, and Act

"I never blame myself when I'm not hitting. I just blame the bat, and if it keeps up, I change bats. After all, if I know it isn't my fault that I'm not hitting, How can I get mad at myself?" Yogi Berra

The wise leader had trained Pete and his partners using the most powerful method available, modeling. Now the question was "do they really get it" or are they just going through the motions. He could see their actions, but had to discover what was motivating and informing their actions- what they were thinking. The wise leader next utilized two powerful methods to tease out and assess the quality of the thinking that was driving their actions and work behavior.

Here's an example of how he did it. All his life Pete had been taught to believe that a certain class of people, another culture, was terrible and hostile, and that he should avoid them at all costs. The wise sage challenged this ideal and coined the golden rule, "the goal of life is to love your neighbor (no matter what culture they are from) as you love yourself." "What!", Pete thought, "I don't even like them. They have weird habits and eat foods that are revolting! What are you thinking?!", he wondered." But because the wise leader had developed a solid relationship with Pete he did allow his thinking to be challenged. He found himself questioning ideas and beliefs that he had held dear and true for years.

Guru-like leaders and Codependent Staff

The wise leader's methods of coaching turned the tables on traditional thinking about training, skill and character development. Most managers believe that it is their job and responsibility to make the employee perform. They continually provide the answers and solutions to their employees problems. By doing so these managers become "the answer Guru" in their staff's eyes. They actually teach their staff to have great confidence in the "fearless" leader, and little confidence in themselves. It's no wonder then, that staff performance is inconsistent. When staff workers try to do the work and come up against a question or problem they can't answer, they must stop and go to the Guru for the answer. In spite of their good intentions, these Guru-like leaders may actually produce a "codependent" staff . This has led to a warped mindset in many employees that the company is out for whatever they can get from me. With a discipleship coaching style, the manager's role is to serve the employee as *they initiate and pursue* their own growth. The contrast in the two leadership styles is shown below.

Type of Leader	Results with People
Guru, Know it all	Dependent on Leader for Performance
Wise Leader	People develop their own Confidence, Skill & Performance

For example, Vince Lombardi, winner of two Super Bowls and the leader who the Super Bowl trophy is named after never let his football players settle for less than the best *they could be.* Lombardi clearly defined the basics of great football- blocking, tackling, catching, quickness, and the right techniques. Instead of constantly telling them how they weren't measuring up, he used questions to help *the players see* where they needed to improve. Great coaches help employees get it. They create an environment where the only thing that can stop the employee progress is the employees himself. The key is to change your focus as a leader and trainer from teaching them how *to* do the job, to *changing the way they are thinking about doing the job,* so that the job can be done right. Let's look now at some of the ways the wise leader did this. He employed two powerful tools:

1. **Thought provoking questions**

2. **Analogic parables that both taught and assessed learning**

Thought-provoking questions that stimulate people's thinking

Let's review thought provoking questions first. Discipleship methodology uses *questions to get at people's thinking* and to develop new neural connections. The wise leader once asked Pete and his buddies the question, "who do people say I am?", to tease out their current knowledge and understanding. Questions like these are classically used in consumer opinion surveys to flesh out the range of their thinking and beliefs on a particular topic by asking "what does/would the average person do or say?" Because he had developed a good relationship them, they answered from their hearts. They replied, 'Some say a great teacher; others say a charismatic leader; and still others, a governor."

This poignant question allowed the wise leader to surface the understanding, and misunderstanding of his fishermen so it could be addressed. He used questions to strategically tease out the learner's level of understanding in order to model the skills at the level that was needed. Like Socrates, here's an example of how the wise leader used a series of questions to gain understanding of a person's existing knowledge. *"And behold, a certain lawyer stood up and tested Him, saying, "Teacher, what shall I do to inherit eternal life?" He said to him, "What is written in the law? What is your reading of it?"* Once the lawyer's existing knowledge was brought to the surface, the astute leader could work with it. What are some of the major benefits of asking a question vs. making a statement?

1) to gain a person's attention,

2) to arouse their interest,

3) to teach a concept,

4) to assess understanding.

The skilled use of observation and questions enables a leader to determine someone's real actions, skills or attitudes. Even the great management teacher Stephen Covey realized the power of questions or queries, vs. telling or sermonizing. Despite the worldwide acclaim for his landmark book *The Seven Habits of Highly Effective People* he wasn't sure his *Seven Habits* seminars were as effective as they could be.[32] His anxieties were confirmed one day as he listened in on people's conversations from a bathroom stall during a break at one of his seminars. He realized that his "bullet point" approach to teaching wasn't reaching the number of people he wanted. Covey has since begun posing more questions which participants to create answers for how they might use his principles to find success in life for themselves-- with much greater effectiveness. *Questions!* You may be thinking. "Why questions? Why don't I just tell them what to do?" When you tell people what to do after you have already told them you fall into two unique traps as a manager.

Trap A: **When you tell them what to do instead of asking a question, this robs you of the chance to really understand the thinking behind their right or wrong behavior.** It is your job to help them *think*, and then act, *correctly*. This cannot happen if you don't clearly understand what they are thinking. Covey states that one must first "seek to understand, then to be understood." Through the skillful art of asking good questions you will be able to discern the thinking, motives and attitudes behind someone's behavior. This will enable you to more effectively give them the exact kind of direction or instruction they need to change their behavior.

Trap B: **When you tell employees what to do instead of asking a question, they don't have to think.** Their brains may not be engaged. This is why many managers are stuck on the merry go round of telling their employees again and again and again the same things- all the while wondering why they didn't get it yet. In order to reinforce what they did right or change the behavior that is off both you, and they, have to be cognizant of their thinking that produced such behavior. By asking a question you activate their minds and this allows them to change their thinking.

| **Trap A** | Assume they don't know existing knowledge | No understanding of their |

| **Trap B** | Tell before asking mind & thinking | Less ability to engage person's |

Bullet Points vs. Value Added Questions

When you are in a room with other managers, what tells you that you are in the presence of a truly professional leader? One answer is how efficiently and effectively they can assess a situation and gather pertinent information to come to a strategic decision, while involving and mentoring people along the way. How much value she or he is able to add to the organization. A great leader gets results through people At the leadership level, what the leader knows is not as important as what "we" know, how much the people in the organization are learning and growing. The key to these goals is the ability to ask good questions.

The "Socratic" method of asking an open ended, non-binary, "yes or no" answer type of question is used by wise leaders to draw out what people are thinking, and allow them to add value. Open ended or essay questions like "Why, What, Who, When, Where and How" types, are used to draw out what people are thinking. Effective leaders are able to lead people to think deeply about their mission and values, beyond a Binary or bullet point understanding . Binary questions are those that only require a "yes" or "no" response. They provide a very limited amount of information to you as a leader. Look at the conversation below, how does the person you are asking feel? How much "value add" is happening through the dialogue about a recent industry conference that both a leader and staff person attended?

Q: "Hava good time at the conference?"

A "Yep, so interesting!"

Q: "Me too, did you enjoy the negotiating to win talk?"

A: "Oh yes, I did." (Yawn, while off on a mental holiday reliving events that were important to them).

Not much value add here. The leader is "validating" what they think is important to make sure the staff person "got it". But what has the leader gained in terms of understanding what the staff person learned? Has the leader provided an opportunity for the staff person to present their "added value" to the organization? Not really.

  The staff person's ability to express and deliver "the mail", the full amount of what they have learned on a subject is limited, by the type of question you, as their fearless leader, have asked. A good question builds people, it can challenge and change character. It indicates a genuine interest in the person, in what they know, and in their value to the organization. When a leader does not thoughtful ask good questions, they lose the opportunity to benefit from all the subordinate's professional knowledge and experience. If a manager continues to simple tell and direct and confirms their own understanding with Binary, yes or no type questions, it won't take long before the subordinate feels "under-valued" and will begin to "clam up." As you'll see below, an Open Ended question can elicit much more information, and allows the person you ask to express their knowledge, but also their perspective and feelings, or doubts on a matter. The person you ask will feel more "empowered" because the Open Ended question allows them to display the "power" of what they know, believe and feel to your benefit. The chart below shows examples of Open Ended questions and contrasting Binary questions on the right:

What is a Good Question?

IS- Opened Ended	IS NOT- Binary
Essay- Where would that competition affect us the most?	**Binary**-That competitor's action would hurt us most in the eastern U.S., right?
Open- How would the introduction of more small sized products affect our margins?	**Closed**- Is the small car trend going to change our business?
Specific- What kind of people with what skills will we need to do the Jones project?	**General**- How are things going?
Knowledge- What features will 20 year olds like?	**Leading**- 20 year olds will like that, right?
Probing- How did the ballgame go?	**Duh**- The ballgame went well, didn't it?
Non Threatening- Who was involved?	**Threatening**- You stupid ___, you did it didn't you!
Drawing- What was your thinking on X decision?	**Defensive**- Why did you react like that?

One note of interest, when you try to use these questions at first you may find that people are silent at first. How come? Because they may not be used to this, are starting to think for themselves, or are pondering what might be the "right thing" to say. Expect more periods of silence, which may seem a bit awkward at first, when you ask questions. When you wait patiently for their answer, you honor them. You demonstrate that you care enough about them to wait and allow them to process their thoughts.

Thought Provoking Question Practice

Here is an exercise to develop the skill of asking thought provoking questions. The idea here is to learn something meaningful or "deep" about someone else that you are in a significant relationship with- at work, home, or in an affinity group (backpacking, painting, opera) by asking thought provoking, open ended, non-binary questions~

1. What do you think about this person? Do you truly, genuinely understand their innate worth and value, and potential. This is designed to surface your current assumptions and thinking about the person. How do you normally view people (as helpers to get things done, evolving beings, deal-withs, weird, slow, brilliant...). One of the things that good leaders do is that they clearly understand the "lense" of how the view people and question their own assumptions and views of others. How you have characterized a person may view how you relate to them, and what kinds of questions or information you expect from them.

_____

2. How will you "jump start" the conversation? What do you have in common? (love being out on the water, war games, strategy) How do you usually ask questions? What question types (see handout) would you like to develop? _____

3. Is there anything in the trainee's heart or mind that you want to be aware of in order to engage them in conversation (i.e., what is their self image or esteem, do they love a challenge or are they more tentative in decision making)? Is there something you wish to test about your approach? What questions do you have about your approach? This will enable you to test your assumptions about people as a leader. For example, you might be thinking, " people may be skeptical, and may not engage me in the conversation. But I hope to "tease

out" a common connection through my use of questions."

---

4. Choose a question type from the Opened Ended question list above and try it out. Record what you thought they would say, and what they actually did. What new understanding did you receive as a result of this exercise? What additional questions did this prompt for you to ask?

Analogic Parables that both Teach and Test

The second method that the wise leader used to both teach and test the understanding of the fishermen was that of telling a special kind of parable. Given the centrality of story in human life and experience, we can begin to appreciate the power and potential of parables for teaching and learning. Rossiter[33] says that the power of story is "deeply appealing and richly satisfying to the human soul, with an allure that transcends cultures, centuries, ideologies, and academic disciplines." Neuhauser[34] explains that stories are effective as teaching tools because they are believable, memorable, and entertaining. Stories are believable when they deal with experiences that people perceive as an authentic and credible in comparison to their own lives. Because many stories offer opportunities to interact with the characters and discover lessons in their lives they invite us to actively make meaning and apply such lessons to our lives. When we hear the story of how a prince like David learns from encounters with lion and a bear to battle a giant enemy like Goliath, we can envision how smaller challenges in life may prepare us for greater ones as well.

For centuries, people have told story-like parables that embodied and enriched their lives. No matter where you live or what language you speak, we all can imagine ourselves as an actor in a story...as the inspired hero, the suffering beauty, the rages to riches immigrant, the misunderstood introvert genius in a well told story. Fishing and hunting stories are told from grandfather to father to son, from uncle to nephew, from sporting club member to new recruit. Grandmothers tell mothers dating and romance stories who tell their daughters, aunts tell nieces and bridge club members all over the world.

ABC/CNN News, blockbuster videos, the latest pop or operatic phenom, and increasing worldwide unrest- so much media is battling for our attention today. Stories or parables provide leaders a way to compete with this media noise. A parable is defined as *something thrown beside something else*; an analogy or comparison. Wise leaders refine their ability to tell earthy stories with powerful, practical truths embedded in them. The wise leader was a master storyteller and question asker. In order to influence people's thinking he would typically ask a question and then relate an analogic parable or story. A parable is a special type of story that accomplishes two very different, yet extremely important goals at once for leaders. In a parable, the wise leader might use a *combination* of inquiry questions, analogy and story, and strategic/confirming questions to assess a person's understanding and motivation for learning. Analogic parables offer special promise for how our brains learn.

Existing Knowledge -- -------	Analogy link ----------- -----	New Knowledge

How Analogic Parables help Brains Learn

As shown in the Figure above, the brain learns through analogies by linking new knowledge to existing knowledge, in the same way that a chain links two different ideas or objects together. If you cannot remember a fact, link it to a meaningful memory and use the latter to hook the former. Analogies follow a form of A is to B as C is to D, where A, B, C, and D are specific numerals, words, or objects. As shown below, the power of the analogy is that in order to understand it, a thinker must induce the relationship between A and B and then transfer, or map, that relationship to C and D (Pellegrino, 1985; Sternberg, 1977; Sternberg & Nigro, 1980).

A is to B   as   **C is to D**

Here are some memorable analogies that help us to understand an unknown-how someone feels or believes based on something that is known. For example, in the salted peanuts example below the uknown (A) is as to the known (B), as the more U.S. troops return home to their families (C) the more their families will want their loved ones to return home (D).

- "Withdrawal of U.S. troops (unknown) will become like salted peanuts (known) to the American public; the more U.S. troops come home, the more will be demanded." - Henry Kissinger in a *Memo to President Richard Nixon*

A is to B   as   **C is to D**

How does this work? Let's map it out

A (troops) are like B (peanuts)

withdrawl of troops is like salted peanuts :   the more troops return

C (the more peanuts you eat, you want more) is like D (wanting more troops)

| the more you eat | the more people will want |
| the more you want | more of their loved ones to return |

desire for more salted peanuts is **like**   tasting my loved ones returning home
once I taste salted peanuts I desire more...   we desire more of our love one...

- "Life (unknown) is like riding a bicycle (known). To keep your balance, you must keep moving." Albert Einstein

Life (A) is like riding a bike (B)   as   balance (C) is like staying in motion (D).

- "People are like stained-glass windows. They sparkle and shine when the sun is out, but when the darkness sets in, their true beauty is revealed only if there is a light from within."

— Elisabeth Kübler-Ross

People (A) are like stained-glass (B) as   light from within (C)   reveals true beauty (D).   .

Now, see if you can fill in the blanks in the next two examples:

- "What sunshine is to flowers, smiles are to humanity. These are but trifles, to be sure; but scattered along life's pathway, the good they do is inconceivable."

— Joseph Addison

Sunshine (A) is to _____ (B)   as   smiles (C) are to _____ (D).

- "truth, like gold, is to be obtained not by its growth, but by washing away from it all that is not gold."

— Leo Tolstoy

Truth (A) like _____ (B)   as   obtained not by _____ (C)   but by _____ (D).

Logical or analogical linkages is the basis of all mnemonic systems. A few people are able to memorize vast amounts of information- entire telephone directories, for example- by using various mnemonic tricks. Memories are groups of neurons that fire together in the same pattern each time they are activated. Whenever you engage your brains' multiple intelligences in *new ways*, for instance, you can grow new circuitry to override your ruts and patterns of thinking. *The ability to develop new circuitry that connects new information to existing information is why analogies are so powerful.*

In order to help you to understand the power of using a parable let me invite you to think about the meaning of an analogic parable through an exercise. One of the wise leader's favorite parables was that of the farmer who went out into his fields to sow seed as presented below.   What do you think he was trying to get at through this parable? Remember, these methods were designed to tease out or challenge existing ideas, beliefs and assumptions, and provide an opportunity to open up a person's mind to learn to think differently.

> The sower went out to sow his seed; and as he sowed, some
> fell beside the road, and it was trampled underfoot and the
> birds of the air ate it up. Other seed fell on rocky soil, and as
> soon as it grew up, it withered away, because it had no
> moisture. Other seed fell among the thorns; and the thorns
> grew up with it and choked it out. Other seed fell into the
> good soil, and grew up, and produced a crop a hundred times
> as great.

How you would you respond to the following questions about the parable above?

As a leader who is communicating with various audiences, what does this parable mean to you?

_____

What does this say about the practice of leadership?

_____

What does it say about followers' responses to leaders?

_____

The telling of this analogic parable reveals several powerful benefits. First, by relating this parable, the leader would have a concrete example to assess the understanding of his followers. In contrast to a T/F or Multiple choice test, the parable is a dynamic story with actors and actions that effectively allows the leader to know what a person learns based upon their responses- much in the same way the questions in the above exercise assessed your understanding of leadership.

Now let's look at the meaning of this parable:

"The sower went out to sow his seed; and as he sowed, some fell beside the road, and it was trampled underfoot and the birds of the air ate it up." The wayside ground was known as the right of way ground between plots of farmland where people walked. This ground was compacted hard as pavement by the feet of countless people. It was therefore highly unlikely that a seed which fell there would take up root.

"Other seed fell on rocky soil, and as soon as it grew up, it withered away, because it had no moisture." Many fields have only a thin skin of dirt over limestone or were chocked with limestone rocks. In this kind of soil a seed would sprout up in the thin top soil, but could not find root and deep moisture to withstand the sun's heat. "Other seed fell among the thorns; and the thorns grew up with it and choked it out." In place the soil had weedy spots, just like almost every other kind of soil in the world. When seed was sown among these, even in good soil, the weeds would grow up to choke out the good plants. "Other seed fell into the good soil, and grew up, and produced a crop a hundred times as great."

Lessons for Leaders from the Parable of the Sower and Seed

What was, and is, the meaning of this parable? For leaders, there are several important lessons. The wise leader chose this parable because as we'll see, his goal was to eventually show the fishermen how to lead so that his movement would be sustainable. First, four different kinds of field soil are described. In how many did the soil "bear fruit"? Only one. This means, through simple arithmetic that the sower was successful with an average of 1 out of 4 seeds, or 25% of the soil in which he sowed. As shown in the figure below, the other 75% of the time the leader and the seed would prove to be unfruitful.

only 25% of the "field" is fertile!

Four Conditions of the Soil

The message was the "seed" the leader was sowing. It had to be very potent, and able to produce fruit. As leaders, this might mean talking about your business mission or opportunity with regards to the fruit it produces. For future recruits this might mean opportunity for income, sales, providing benefits for the family and retirement, customer satisfaction, stock bonuses, bettering society or the environment, or changing the world for good- depending on what "fruit" is meaningful to the potential recruit.

The four types of soil are also helpful descriptions of what happens in life. Some people are simply not open to your message at all, they are not a good "fit" and have motivations that differ from yours as a leader- these would represent the "beside the road" soil and reject the message and opportunity.

The other two types, rocky or thorny, are similar. Over time, after working with different recruits, a leader who was also a learner would start to recognize typical "rocks or thorny issues" that cropped up consistently with recruits. The leader might hear things like "what if you and I disagree about a plan of action", "what if a customer is picky or in a bad mood", "sometimes I like to take the day off and go to the beach, okay?" These may represent the classic warning signs that it is time to end the interview with a potential recruit.

In this example, the mind or heart of person is compared by analogy to the hard ground in the parable. The hard ground could represent someone's defensiveness or a closed attitude to new ideas, which makes them slow to receive a leader's inspiration. Either way, this results in an impervious surface that is not open to learning or growth. Trying to teach a person like this might be like talking to a proverbial "brick wall"-- the rocky, shallow soil. Their motivation or commitment is shallow. So when the tests and trials come, and they invariably do, the person may lose interest and quit. Perhaps the largest lessons though, are: 1) "where should the leader focus their efforts on recruiting" and 2) "how can the leader work through the inevitable rejection and discouragement that come with the first three types of soil"?

A growing leader might want to be involved in a network with more experienced, seasoned leaders who could provide them with the kind of perspective and wisdom that only come from trial and error experience. These seasoned leaders could provide reassurance of what is "par for the course" in working with people, helping to pull the younger leader out a potential pit of despair or discouragement. Over time, a leader would be able to identify or see the "poor investment of my time and energy" recruit coming. They also would be able to identify the high potential 30-, 60- or 90-fold return recruit, whose network of friends and associates may include others like her or him. The leader might develop qualifying questions or mechanisms that would allow them to "weed out" (pun intended) people that do not represent the type of soil that would offer a strong future return.

You might imagine the same kind of parable used in a different context. How about with a sales manager communicating the challenges of selling to some new hires who were going out on their first sales calls. The manager could have simply stated the bottom line, saying, "it's a numbers game, you will invariably have to get over rejection of people who don't buy." But instead, by using a parable a potential new salesperson can picture themselves going out and selling product. They can envision people as the different types of soil and perhaps over time they would also begin to learn signs that would tell them in advance what kind of prospect person X might be- hard, rocky, subject to birds, or fertile. As a new person was starting out in sales and learning the potential red flags and warning signs of bad soil, he or she would invariably make some bad hires or bad decisions which would prove unfruitful later. How would the person work through the emotional toll, discouragement and sense of failure that he or she would experience?

The Hidden Assessment Value of the Analogic Parable

Perhaps the greatest value of relating an analogic parable instead of giving people the bottom line is that they may not completely understand it at first, and then ask questions that show what their level of understanding is. In this way the parable's benefits are seen not just as a teaching tool but *as a method of assessment*. The leader, or experienced sales manager, knows the kinds of questions that typically will surface about the parable as it relates to leadership or sales. And hence, if a recruit does, or conversely does not, ask a certain question this will provide valuable information about how the person views the issue of leadership or sales. For example, does a growing leader realize that their wonderful new ideas or vision may not be accepted by all the people they communicate to at first? How will they deal with this discouragement and disappointment?

The same might be said for a new salesperson who thinks- and rightly so- that their Fuller brushes are the highest quality brushes in the entire world. And hence has difficulty understanding why everyone wouldn't want to buy one? Or is so fearful to approach a potential customer that she or he doesn't realize that there are a few high potential "fertile" folks who, once they experience the brush quality, will tell all their friends and sell them on the salesperson's behalf.

Effective analogic parables typically do not impose anything and do not threaten the listener at first since they are designed to both provoke and assess thought. Unlike traditional leaders who command, tell, or control their followers, analogic parables provide a much different way of achieving leadership. Because they do not put the listener on the defensive and are intriguing, they may be able to overcome many natural resistance and self-defence mechanisms, appealing to them through the practical, everyday items of life people can relate to. Analogic parables offer a type of indirect message that has more chance to be accepted that a direct rebuke. To say "It is not the healthy who need a doctor, but the sick" is wiser and more tactful than saying, for example, "This is not an area where we need to be involved"…

The best parables can be constructed in order to provide an opportunity reveal the truth to those *who really want to know it* (which is shown by the further questions they arouse), and to conceal the truth from men of casual curiosity or motivation. And this may be one of their primary benefits. Analogic parables, because they do not speak directly to a situation, may offer a unique method of testing the motivations of the listener. Followers who really wish to understand and pursue knowledge from a leader will ask questions and test their understanding. Those who are not motivated to learn and grow will not. In this way, the leader may assess the true motivations, and current understanding, of the followers without issuing them a 200 question multiple choice exam.

Key Benefits of Analogic Parables

The wise leader used analogic parables with great effect. Here is a summary of their benefits:

1. Analogic parables were designed to hide revelation and understanding from those who were not interested or motivated to learn. What for? Think about the Parable of the Sower. Effective leaders understand that they must first qualify their people to see if they are worth the investment. True discipleship requires a significant investment of time and resources. The wise leader was not willing to invest that in people who were not sincerely interested in following, and being mentored. Some of the people, like the different kinds of soil, will be more or less motivated to follow the leader. The people who are truly interested and worthy of investment will respond to analogic parables by asking questions or probing for understanding.

2. He taught people something they did not yet know, by comparing to something they did know. His stories or parables enabled people to understand things they did not know, by comparing them to things they did. The telling of the parable invited a response, from those who were interested and motivated to learn. For example, the wise leader once told an analogic parable likening his new organization to a mustard tree seed. While the complexities of his new organization may not have been easy to grasp, some people could understand the potential of a tiny mustard seed to grow into a large tree. They had seen such growth and could associate with it. The wise leader sowed out stories just like little seeds on the soil of people's hearts. Interestingly, sometimes the parables did not yield "fruit" immediately. The fishermen did not do or understand what the wise leader wanted them to

immediately after he communicated the stories. However, they did "get it" as the stories were reinforced through the example and modeling of his life. When a seed is planted in someone's life, and it is watered through some kind or repetition or reinforcement, it may grow bigger and bigger until it becomes great and useful.

3.   Parables use analogies to make abstract, conceptual ideas concrete. Few people can grasp abstract or the theoretical ideas. People think more concretely. "Seeing is believing." And people may see and understand more clearly through pictures. We could talk about fidelity in terms of theory all day, or we could read a story of how King Ulysses was away at sea for 90 years, and how his wife Penelope remained faithful to him even though pursued by relentless suitors in The Book of Virtues.[35]   We easily recognize the virtue of both the King and wife in remaining true to each other.   Analogic stories help us put flesh on understanding, ideas and thinking. The last great benefit of an analogy is that it helps people to think for themselves.   An effective teacher does not do the thinking for his students.   Analogies help people to make their own deductions and to discover the truth for themselves. Truth can have a powerful impact when it is a personal discovery. Wise leaders do not wish to save people the mental sweat of thinking, but desire to compel them *to think.*

Keys to Create an effective Analogic Parable

Here are a few tips to enable you to create effective analogic parables:.

1. **Tell the parable about something you and your audience are familiar with**. Let's say you like rowing and wanted to a particularly strong headed member of your team on the subject of considering others.   You could talk about the need to "sync" your stroke with the other in the boat, even if you are stronger and more powerful, so that whole boat moves more powerful. If you

are out of sync with your teammates in the boat, your powerful stroke may be wasted because their weight shift and stroke will be moving in the opposite direction. Or let's say you love the opera and you were working with someone who kept "doing their own thing" and not listening to the goals of the team or your directions as a leader. You might talk about the need for the orchestra and the singers to understand and perform together according to a common score. If any orchestra piece, plays out of tune, or if an opera primadona holds her note too long or too short so that she is out of sync with the orchestra this sticks out like a sore thumb.

2. **Make an Emotional Connection to Gain and Hold Attention.** Parables have power when they are constructed to engage and make emotional connection or analogy between what we need to know and what we already know.[36] The wise leader made this connection with two steps: (1) He told a story that dramatically brought out some striking feature of human experience. We see something surprising or ironic or shrewd or inspiring or outrageous. The sower went out into the field with the hope of sowing seed to produce a crop, but got poor results at first. Because he used situations his audience was familiar with those who were motivated and willing to learn with question or comment with something like, "Yes, that is surprising/shrewd/ outrageous/whatever, isn't it?" (2) Then the leader may either draw out the analogy by telling another parable or ask a thought provoking question that will allow the follower to figure out the analogy for themselves. In the rowing parable with the powerful personality above you might say, "you might think that the most powerful rowers win the race, but that's not the whole story..." to tease out their think on how power needs to be synced up with others.

3. **Elaborately "encode" your parable with analogies- actors and villains, events, drama, and elements that your audience can relate to.** The key is to elaborately tell the story with actors, drama, and consequences so that the

listener can link your message to their existing knowledge and experience. How? By using analogies. Human knowledge grows by moving from what we *do understand to what we don't understand*. The person who gives an analogy is like a trailblazer who sees what's up ahead, with knowledge of the terrain that those behind can't yet share. One of the best ways to do this is to imagine an describe the new learning in terms *of what it is like, in terms that they already know.* For example, "Well, you'll find there's a ditch to jump to get to your destination, but heck, it's no bigger than that one back at Miller's Crossing." Parables help the audience understand something new when it is compared or "thrown down next to" something which we are already familiar with. Is as if a Tesla pulled up to a Ford truck at a stop light. The leader might say, "These two autos are like each other in some ways and in other ways they are very different." The follower who is motivated by price would respond, "Yes, one costs about 70k!" The leader would then know some valuable clues about the person and their motivations, without asking a direct question. To a hesitant, insecure and fearful person, the wise leader might say: "It is difficult to plow a field while looking back at the same time. If you really want to go forward, stop looking through the rear-view mirror." This type of indirect message has a greater chance of being accepted that a direct rebuke.

4. **Next, introduce a thought provoking point, twist to the story, a hero, or element that stimulates thought or interest.** This is a major benefit of the parable, to assess understanding, or provoke reflection on the part of the listener. The twist is specifically designed to get the listener to think and to respond, if they are interested and motivated to do so. In the parable of the person sowing seed above, most people who have planted peas or tomatoes in their backyard would normally expect good results, good fruit. However, the point of learning is that real life is that way. In the backyard garden we can control all the conditions, soil, plant placement for light and heat, fertilizer, etc.

When dealing with real people in real life, we cannot control all the conditions, and hence may experience failure. This unexpected twist may cause the listener to probe more deeply into their thinking about leadership.

5. **Lastly, add a thought-provoking question that may cause your audience to reflect more deeply on what you are trying to get them to learn.** We have gone through this exercise in the previous sections of this chapter by asking questions like "what does the parable of the sower teach us about leadership?" By asking a question the audience's current understanding and knowledge will surface. And then you, as a leader, can more effectively reinforce what they know that is correct, and teach further to areas of need.

6

Joy and Skill Producing Assignments that Teach and Test

"Think? How the hell are you gonna think and hit at the same time?"

Yogi Berra

For the next phase in the development of the fishermen, the wise leader created a very special kind of assignment designed to both test their knowledge, skills and attitudes, and to provide further opportunity for learning. Unfortunately, this methodology is not the kind that most new recruits receive with their first assignments. Many newcomers find themselves with an assignment that they have neither the skill nor inclination to succeed at. They are "thrown into the deep end of a pool when they have not yet learned to swim, and do not even wish to." Ineffective managers simply put them in their job role and let them find their own way, with little forethought or strategy as to how and what might assist their development on the job.

Assignments that are designed to satisfy both customer and employees are all too rare in today's workplace, and this is costing corporations a lot of money. Certainly, most managers would design assignments to achieve the first goal of satisfying the customer. But despite the considerable amount of research that show a strong link that happy employees truly do produce happy customers, much of corporate America is failing in this regard. A survey by Right Management[37] of 411 workers in the U.S. and Canada showed that only 19% were satisfied with their jobs. Another 16% said they were "somewhat satisfied." But the rest, nearly two-thirds of respondents, indicated they were unhappy at work. A recent Gallup study indicated that disengaged employees cost the U.S. economy $370 billion annually in lost productivity[38].

In additional to joyful outcomes, the right assignments develop skill and competency. At the General Electric Company, the only company originally listed on the New York Stock Exchange that still survives today, leaders devote enormous energy to matching key managers with the right assignments in order to develop their potential. G.E.'s spends about $1 billion annually on training, but doesn't use a great deal of canned course work to magically produce leaders. Ultimately the purpose of G.E.'s Crotonville School is to transmit G.E.'s values to employees. Steve Kerr[39], a former director of the school, explained: "I wish I could tell you that courses are the key, but they are not. When we ask our people to write down the outstanding development experience of their lives, only about 10% cite formal training." The majority of peak learning experiences occur on the job- and through real life work experiences, not through lectures or formal teaching. Kerr recommends developing a series of *varied and challenging work assignments* characterized by lots of responsibility and real risk of failure.

Anatomy of an Effective Assignment

The wise leader's assignments were strategically designed to provide the opportunity to accomplish multiple goals of customer satisfaction and employee satisfaction or joy, while developing key skills in the new recruits. Here is the "anatomy" of a strategically constructed assignment. The first step in an effective assignment is to think strategically. Here is the first skill producing assignment that the wise leader gave his new recruits. What key aspects of attitude, character and skills do you think he was trying to produce as you read this "assignment"?

> The wise leader sent his recruits `out into the marketplace saying: "Go out in teams of two. Do talk to the locals and do not try to sell to people from a foreign culture. Go to the local people we know best first. Sell them by saying, "an entirely

new way of doing business is now available for you." Show them by actually building new business for them, growing leaders, getting people out of bad habits. Model for them, show them the way. Don't take a large expense account with you, for a good worker is worthy of his food. Now whatever city or town you enter, inquire who in it is a good person, and invest in and honor them. Network with them until you go on to another town... If the person is worthy of your investment, you will learn how to discern this over time. And whoever will not receive you nor hear your words, when you depart from that house or city leave the rejection you feel behind you.

Here's how this assignment was strategically designed to develop multiple areas of expertise and attitudes in the hearts and minds of the fishermen in key customer, skill, and team areas :

1. **Customer- Enabled them to succeed with a certain kind of people or customer in mind, and have a low/medium degree of challenge.** They were called to reach customers they were more familiar with, not foreigners which would have been much harder to do.

2. **Skill- Provided the opportunity to test and enhance understanding and growth in specific areas of expertise.** The assignment was designed to develop specific skills in the recruits (growing leaders, sales, negotiation, conflict resolution, service) in a "kill several birds with one stone" assignment.

3. **Team Development- Provided opportunities for "rough edges" relational development.** Since they were sent out in teams of two they could "work things out" over time. Perhaps one of them snored, or had bad manners, or talked too loudly, or was too assertive-- all these "rough relational edges" could be worked on. Opportunities for relational development could include

relationship to superiors or authority, to customers, to peers, to subordinates, to team members. In what relational areas does they need to develop? After several days of working together in the same place people's bad habits may have begun to surface! The opportunity here would be the acceptance of feedback from peers and the ability to let ones guard down so two-way conversation can flow freely and willingly amongst all parties involved.

4. Honoring Relationships- fostered a culture of honor and respectful relationships. In contrast to other business paradigms that focus on profitability and get rich quick schemes, discipleship is characterized by long term relationships that are marked by honor. By finding a good person who is worthy of investment and honor, the value of an individual is upheld. People receive respect and recognition, and may tend to reciprocate. A powerful network of honoring, like minded individuals is the intended result.

5. Working through rejection- the assignment helped the fishermen work through an inevitable sense of rejection that they would experience in their first "sales" assignment. One of the first things that any salesperson must understand and work through is the sense of rejection that comes with the territory. The assignment was designed with the expectation that rejection would happen and gave a provision for how to deal with it.

By designing assignments that focused on key areas of skill development with a degree of challenge that was incrementally greater than whatever level of skill they had achieved before, the wise leader enabled his staff to succeed. The power of an incrementally greater level goal for skill development Vgotsky[40] called the zone of proximal

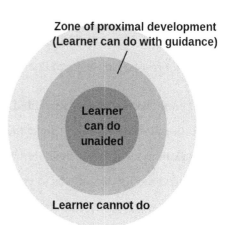

**Zone of proximal development
(Learner can do with guidance)**

**Learner
can do
unaided**

Learner cannot do

development. The idea is that there is a "zone" between what the learner can and cannot do where the assignment provides the opportunity for improvement. For example, each January, over 100,000 General Electric employees and their bosses communicate about the skills, career goals, and development needs to create a plan that will take each person, and G.E., to the next level of success. Between March and May, senior executives visit each of G.E.'s 12 operating units to conduct highly focused one-day personnel reviews that show how the assignments are progressing, or not. Meeting mainly with the top leadership at each site, they end up considering the prospects of about 500 G.E. senior managers for future leadership positions, and the assignments that could help them reach the next level.

The following table matrix may help you "fill in the blanks" for what constitutes an effective assignment. Remember, the outcome of an effective assignment should achieve skill development, customer results, and employee satisfaction and joy as discussed on above. The table is filled in for the fisherman's assignment as a representative example. A blank table appears at the end of this chapter.

Assignment Design	Skill Development	Customer Results	Employee Satisfaction & Joy
Teams of two	Cooperation, teamwork, relational development	Health and Long life	Friendship, Mission accomplishment, fulfillment

Deliberate Practice makes Perfect

The phrase "practice makes perfect", while catchy, is fiction. Deliberate, perfect practice makes perfect! What are the necessary ingredients for perfect, deliberate practice? The need for and benefits of mentoring and internship programs for the development of people have been well established in the literature since the introduction of Benjamin Bloom's (1985) foundational work, *Developing Talent in Young People[41]*. Bloom studied virtuoso pianists and sculptors, Olympic swimmers, research scientists, champion tennis players. Ericsson[42] noted, "Elite performers in many diverse domains have been found to practice, on the average, roughly the same amount every day, including weekends." Bloom and Ericsson found that study with devoted teachers or mentors, the amount and quality of deliberate practice, and appropriate balances of challenging tasks with support are important factors in the development of talent.

In a study of 20-year-old violinists by Ericsson and colleagues, the best group (judged by conservatory teachers) averaged 10,000 hours of deliberate practice over their lives; the next-best averaged 7,500 hours; and the next, 5,000. The same results can be demonstrated in studies that looked at top surgeons, musicians, salesmen and professional athletes. Perfect, deliberate practice equals better performance. And the more of it, the better. In Colvin's[43] book "Talent is Overated: What Really Separated World-class Performers from Everybody Else", he reviews hundreds of studies on how people achieved great performance and found that the best people in any field are those who devoted the most hours to what researchers call "deliberate practice." In deliberate practice, mentors define skill and attitude objectives just beyond one's current level of competence, provide feedback on results and inspire high levels of repetition. Colvin provides this example from the game of golf:

> Simply hitting a bucket of balls is not deliberate practice,
> which is why most golfers don't get better. Hitting an eight-
> iron 300 times with a goal of leaving the ball within 20 feet of
> the pin 80 % of the time, in the presence of a master who

observes results and models appropriate adjustments, and
doing that for hours every day - that's deliberate practice.

Thus, investing time in designing the right kind of skill-producing assignment that enables people to deliberately practice on exactly the right things may be one of the most important functions of a wise leader.

Designing Skill-Producing Assignments for Deliberate Practice

John Wooden, UCLA basketball coaching legend who won a record 10 national titles, provides a great example of the importance of designing skill and character producing assignments and deliberate practice. Wooden never focused his players on the end result of winning the game. He wanted them to fully concentrate each moment on the fundamentals of what they were doing at the time. Focusing on developing key skills- dribbling quickly, passing accurately, blocking out and leaping for the rebound in a certain way, and shooting precisely through deliberate practice. He knew that when his players mastered all these skills, the wins would follow- and several championships were won as a result. Wooden[44] designed assignments for deliberate practice to train his team in what he called a "pyramid of success". The pyramid contained elements of character like industriousness and enthusiasm as cornerstones. Several skills areas like cooperation and poise were also highlighted. For example, a typical practice was scripted like this, to accomplish cooperation:

3:40-3:45: Five-man rebounding and passing.

3:45-3:50: Five-man dribble and pivot.

3:50-4:00: Five-man alternative post pass and cut options.

4:00-4:15: Three-man lane with one and two men alternating on defense, parallel lane, weave pivot, front and side.

If people are to deliver great results, they must develop consummate skills. In order to hit a home run, one must be able to hit the ball with power. Many managers set high goals for their employees without addressing the critical area of skill development. This is like picking a man off the street, and asking him to hit a home run out of a major league ball park. Unless the manager is very fortunate, the man will not have the skill to hit a ball 380 feet. Yet many companies expect such performance without addressing the need for skill development or training. The popular saying in major league baseball "Just win baby!" tells the story. Many managers focus their staff strictly on results, and in so doing, will not be able to achieve the best outcomes. Research has shown that people tend to deliver greater results when they focus on mastering skills, instead of producing results.[45] The wonderful story of the Olympic gold medal eight man rowing team in the book "The Boys in The Boat" had developed the capacity for oxygen intake, a skill that only elite rowers possess, through hours of deliberate practice:

> A well-conditioned oarsman or oarswoman competing at the highest levels must be able to take in and consume as much as eight liters of oxygen per minute; an average male is capable of taking in roughly four to five liters at most. Pound for pound, Olympic oarsmen may take in and process as much oxygen as a thoroughbred racehorse. This extraordinary rate of oxygen intake is of only so much value, it should be noted. While 75–80 percent of the energy a rower produces in a two-thousand-meter race is aerobic energy fueled by oxygen, races always begin, and usually end, with hard sprints. These sprints require levels of energy production that far exceed the body's capacity to produce aerobic energy, regardless of oxygen intake. Instead the body must immediately produce.

World class coach George Yeoman Pocock described the leadership skill required to produce elite rowers this way. "Rowing is perhaps the toughest of sports. Once the race starts, there are no time-outs, no substitutions. It calls upon the limits of human endurance. The coach must therefore impart the secrets of the special kind of endurance that comes from mind, heart, and body.[46]" How many of your employees have an "I'm not going to and you can't make me attitude"? How many are "agreeing with you on the outside", but you know that they are "fighting you on the inside"? If you are truly going to have a great company of people that work together the way you want them to, they must have the right attitudes or values. This is why the earlier chapter on recruiting through observation is so important. The people in every great organization are distinguished by their people's attitudes.

Think about it. The 1990 San Francisco 49ers- professionalism, Walmart-friendliness, Nordstrom- personal service. Defining key attitudes will help you to find the right people in which to invest your training. They are important not only for serving your customer, but for healthy team and individual relationships as well. Current research shows that the right attitudes can significantly affect learning. Attitudes like fair mindedness and openness to evidence on any issue; respect for opinions that differ from one's own; inquisitiveness and a desire to be informed; a tendency to reflect before acting and numerous others have been shown to significantly enhance learning.[47]

The Satisfaction and Joy Experienced showed they were the Right People for the Job

The wise leader designed a strategic assignment to provide an opportunity to both train and test his new recruits to serve people, and in turn they received two huge benefits: skill and satisfaction. Each instruction given in the assignment was designed to test a key skill that he had modeled for them previously, and provide an opportunity to learn it more deeply through personal experience. He would then go to the cities and people that Pete and his peers had visited in order to see how well they passed their "exams" and give them constructive feedback on where they succeeded and where to improve. Like a multifunction Swiss army knife, these assignments were designed to develop skill, satisfy customers, and to increase job satisfaction and joy of employees as shown in the figure below.

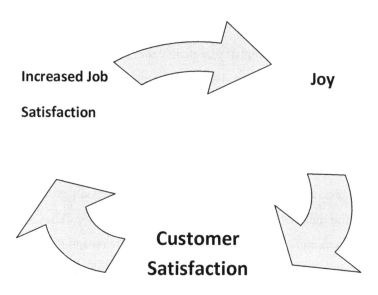

Increased Job Satisfaction

Joy

Customer Satisfaction

"That was amazing!", Pete said. "Lots of people were interested our way of doing business. They loved us. They invited us to their family BBQs. Wow, this stuff almost sells itself! Plus, I actually learned a ton about the partner who you sent me out with. We discovered so many creative, new ways to approach people. Of course, we had a few disagreements at first. But we worked them out, and now we're best friends!" Because the assignments were so well designed, Pete and his peers experienced great success and fruitfulness in their completion. And found, to their surprise, that they were enjoying working for the wise leader immensely. The fact that they did experience joy and satisfaction *further confirms that they were the right people for the job.*

The importance of Joy in the Brain

Our brains are designed to experience joy and satisfaction[48]. A sense of joy and mirth develops as infants when our parents smile and rejoice over us. Babies learn to mimic their parents smiles and joy, which develops what is called the "joy center" in their brains. As we experience joy and job satisfaction at work, our mood elevates and this can have a positive effect on customer satisfaction as well. The remarkable power of joy on people's emotional and personal satisfaction has been documented in the psychological literature as early as 1916[49]. Employee satisfaction produces positive effects on cognitive and behavioral enhancement, positive emotions about work[50]. These effect have been found across different cultures and age groups. According to Gallup studies[51] show that businesses with higher employee satisfaction also garner:

• 86% higher customer ratings
• 76% more success in lowering turnover
• 70% higher profitability
• 78% better safety records

NCAA and Super Bowl champion winning coach Pete Carroll of the Seattle Seahawks is known for his ability to develop more "ordinary" free agent rookie players who were not selected in the NFL draft. Carroll and his staff were able to both observe these ordinary rookies and to develop 11 free agents into key contributors that helped to take the team to the Super Bowl in 2014. One of the key elements in their development is the design the kind of strategic assignments that allowed them to "experience early successes". Just like the wise leader, Carroll first observed the rookies at their training try outs and then put them into situational assignments in which they can have success in their areas of strength, to show them what they can do, and to build a sense of success and confidence. For example, Carroll limited the complexity of pass routes for first year quarterback Russell Wilson. In the second year, Carroll released more and more complex assignments that Wilson was able to progressively master, taking the Seahawks to the Super Bowl, and a sense of incredible joy of satisfaction for a job well done.

Progressively Difficult Assignments with Constructive Feedback

Harvard Business School Professor Bowers[52] (2007) analyzed 1800 leadership successions and found that companies performed significantly better when they groomed insiders for the job of CEO. His research suggests the following practices for developing leaders which reinforce many of the concepts we've already presented. High potential executives are worked through increasingly difficult assignments and rigorous mentoring feedback sessions. Here are some of the assignment practices he found from the successful organizations:

• Hire people of potential and give them ample opportunities to rise to the top: Hire from a diverse pool of highly talented individuals who have general manager potential. Over time, they'll become good insiders, learning from various assignments and projects to manage in the context of the company's strategy, systems, and culture.

• Grow and groom potential leaders from the inside of the company: Hand them increasingly complex assignments that ready them to manage a whole business as early as possible. This is a long, intensive process which should begin by the time they're age thirty.

• Mentor: Assign senior managers to oversee inside-outsiders' development. These mentors help protégés extract lessons from each assignment and ensure that there are adequate (but not excessive) resources for protégés to turn new ideas into great business.

How Deliberate Practice and Constructive Feedback Changes the Brain

Because our brains are plastic they are able to learn and change. Learning in the brain occurs when the connection strengths between neurons are modified when we focus our attention on something we want to learn.[53] What we focus on or practice is what we learn. The axiom "practice makes perfect" is true, when we practice perfectly. Colvin chronicles multiple studies that show what explains the difference between ordinary and extraordinary performers in his book Talent is Overrated[54]. The number one factor that explains great performance is called deliberate practice. Deliberate practice involves the understanding of what skills are necessary to develop to achieve greatness, relentless practice on developing those skills, and continuous feedback on the results of the practice. However, one must first know what to practice on-- what is good and right in order to change in the right direction. Like a golfer who continues to practice and reinforce bad putting technique, we may continually reinforce what is incorrect and hence grow bad connections in our brains. This is where the role of the teacher or mentor is so highly important and valued. A survey of 81 managers focused on constructive feedback[55] shows that the feedback is effective and constructively received. Here's how they characterized what was effective and constructive feedback:

- focuses on identifiable problems and behaviors upon which I can take action
- suggests that my weaknesses can be overcome or remedied
- makes reference to clear, legitimate standards for acceptable behavior
- is very specific and detailed
- makes reference to specific situations or incidents that are problematic
- makes clear reference to the behaviors that I need to fix

Award winning coach John Wooden's feedback was marked by short, punctuated, and numerous one liners. There were *no* lectures, *no* extended harangues. Although frequent and often in rapid-fire order, his utterances were very distinct yet Wooden rarely spoke longer than 20 seconds.   Most of what he said could be categorized as "Compliments, Instructions or Corrections." Compliments were equally balanced with corrections:

"Take lots of shots in areas where you might get them in games."

"Do some dribbling between shots."

"Don't walk."

"Hard driving, quick steps."

Neural networks in our brains must be trained correctly and skillfully to biologically change into a new, desired state. When a mentor provides a learner with sound feedback and direction, the right kind of learning can occur because errors or inaccuracies in thinking are confronted and redirected. Since deliberate practice and feedback is so important in achieving great

performance, it is vitally important to know what to practice on. This is where most people run into trouble. One their own they can rarely see exactly where they need to make a change in focus to improve. The discipleship paradigm combines the right kind of incrementally challenging assignments, deliberate practice and constructive feedback, like the climber who conquers successively higher mountains

with an experienced guide, that creates incremental improvement in skill, results, and confidence.

Listen to this example of how Cy Young winning big league pitcher Nolan Ryan helped a a fellow pitcher Randy Johnson[56] to also win the Cy Young award five times. The two power pitchers talked when the Rangers visited

Seattle in 1992. Johnson said, "Ryan gave me a tip on my foot positioning on my windup that made all the difference in my delivery. He walked me through his thinking on how to set up batters, never really giving up on them. *His message was simple: Cut down on your walks, cut down your base runners, and you have a better chance of winning.* As I practiced what he told me I gained momentum and confidence on the mound." In the 20 games that followed his talk with Ryan, Johnson's record improved to 11-5, with a 2.79 earned run average, and 10.68 strikeouts per game.

Here are some examples of ideas, and a blank table, to help you create assignments that develop people's patterns of thinking and skill, satisfy customers, and produce satisfaction and joy.

1. Design a level of challenge and support- The first assignment was designed to enable them to reach a customer type that they were familiar with- their own people, not foreigners (Samaritans) which would have been much easier to do. Enable the them to succeed with a certain kind of people or customer in mind, and have a low/medium degree of challenge. As they develop, increase the level of challenge.

_____

_____

2. Design the assignment to develop specific skills. What are your people current skill levels? Think about what skills you need to develop (sales, negotiation, conflict resolution, service) and specific ways or drills (negotiation, project management) to develop these skills for your assignment.

_____

_____

3. Teamwork- Provide opportunities for "rough edges" relational development. Opportunities for relational development could include relationship to superiors or authority, to customers, to peers, to subordinates, to team members. In what relational areas does the them need to develop? Design the assignment to test these areas.

_____

_____

4. Reality- Communicate a clear picture of the "brutal facts" or "tough realities" of the business or situation. Effective leaders do not "sugar coat" anything. We live in "dog eat dog, brutal realities" world. Prepare your people for it.

_____

_____

5. Risk/Reward- Think about the concept of reward that was covered in chapter 2. What might motivate your them to pursue the assignment with full commitment, like The Boys in the Boat. Some questions you might want to consider are, " Is the reward worth it? Does it involve elements that are more intrinsic, like the pride of simply mastering a skill for its own sake, like the Japanese tea ceremony?" Or is the individual more interested in an extrinsic reward system, like an annual reward and recognition program, or some form of compensation or promotion.

_____

_____

6. **Constructive Feedback-** what opportunities for constructive feedback can you design to provide key feedback about the effectiveness of their performance on an assignment:

_____

_____

A helpful table that will enable you to "cover the bases" and design effective assignments appears below:

Assignment Design	Skill Development	Customer Results	Employee Satisfaction & Joy
Project			
Meeting			
Sales Call			
Difficult Situation			
Challenging Customer			

7

Final Exam- Creating extraordinary people- who create extraordinary people- who create extraordinary people- who change the world...

How do you change your world? By changing the life of one person at a time. And, further, by teaching them how to reproduce "themselves", to teach them how to change the life of another, and so on. By applying the ancient paradigm of discipleship in your world today, you learn how to observe, test, recruit and train the right people with the right kind of skills that make all the difference. Because of this ability in reproduction, the discipleship paradigm appears to offer more promise than both transactional or even transformation leadership paradigms. In transactional leadership, the focus is on "tit for tat" or compensation for tasks performed. For example, one might pay a construction worker $200 per 250 square foot of finished space, so the focus is on the transaction. In transformational leadership, the goal is the transformation of the construction worker's skill, and attitudes to achieve 500 square feet of finished space for the $200. Transformational leadership is akin the "teach a man to fish" analogy. If you give a man a fish you have fed him for the day. If you teach a man to fish you have fed him for a lifetime.

The focus of the leader is to transform the person, but does not teach them how to transform another. Discipleship goes beyond these two paradigms. Through it, productive tasks result and people are transformed. And this transformation is designed to both impact the person, a multiple generations of people after them. The shared experience of the 1936 eight man Olympic rowing team taught and transformed every person on the team:

...taught us about survival, about overcoming difficulty, about
prevailing over adversity, but it also taught us something about
the underlying reason for surviving in the first place.
Something about infinite beauty, about undying grace, about
things larger and greater than ourselves. About the reasons we
were all here... The challenges they had faced together had
taught them humility—the need to subsume their individual
egos for the sake of the boat as a whole—and humility was the
common gateway through which they were able now to come
together and begin to do what they had not been able to do
before.

The same could be said for Andy Dorrance, Judy Foudy, April Heinrichs, Joy
Fawcett and Mia Hamm who changed the state of women's soccer through the
1996 Olympic team, and millions of young women soccer players after them.
Or for John Wooden, who forever changed the character of NCAA Division 1
men's basketball. Or for Bill Walsh, whose mark will be ever felt on the
National Football league, forever, through the coaches he developed directly,
and in turn, the coach they developed.

Their focus went beyond simply the transformation of a person. Through
their relationship with the leader an individual learned how to transform others,
who in turn, could transform others, generation after generation. Using the fish
analogy, discipleship teaches a man how to fish and how to teach another to
fish, thus changing a generation, and another generation, and changing the
world. The differences in the three leadership paradigms is shown in the chart
below.

Paradigm	Focus	People Influenced
Transactional	Productive Tasks	👤
Transformational	Productive Tasks, Skill Development	👤
Discipleship	Productive Tasks, Skill Development, Teaching Others the same...	👤 👤 👤 👤 👤 👤 👤 👤 👤 👤 👤 ,,,,,

How did the wise leader accomplish the difficult task of discipleship?   Here is a timeline that recaps the sequence of Discipleship Methods and key outcomes. The sequence is important and like building blocks is constructed layer by layer over time.

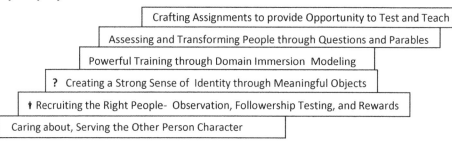

Crafting Assignments to provide Opportunity to Test and Teach

Assessing and Transforming People through Questions and Parables

Powerful Training through Domain Immersion Modeling

? Creating a Strong Sense of Identity through Meaningful Objects

⭡ Recruiting the Right People- Observation, Followership Testing, and Rewards

Caring about, Serving the Other Person Character

Time ⟶

The foundation for the discipleship paradigm is that of caring and servant of others leadership. People don't care how much you know until *they know how much you care*. Next, a combination of observation, tests, and rewards was used to recruit the right kind of people to invest in, and to test their "followership" capacity. Next, he defined a new identity for his recruits using real life, tangible objects that they could relate to. Using Meaningful objects the wise leader created a powerful new identity in the fishermen that radically changed *how they viewed themselves* and *their purpose for living in the world.* The wise leader went beyond a traditional "arms-length" relationship with his followers to develop the kind of caring relationship that was to significantly influence the development of his followers' identity and social identity. The wise leader modeled what he had learned firsthand, what was vital to lives of the listeners, not merely what he had learned in books. He taught things that would change people's lives not merely enlightened them. The wise leader developed skills that dramatically improved their lives, and enabled them to also dramatically serve others and to improve their lives as well.

Most other leaders of the day were content to act like a "genius with 1,000 helpers" who were charged with accomplishing a grand mission. They taught men to achieve their grand mission. They "taught them how to fish." Their followers achieved great results in the short term- won wars, built large economies, expanded trade with other nations, and they died. And their movements died with them. The wise leader, however, went beyond merely teaching his followers "how to fish" in his unique mission and values. This extraordinary leader taught them how to fish, but went further, teaching them how to teach others how to fish. In this way, a growing number of people-generation after generation after generation would change, thus changing the world.

Discipleship and The Apprenticeship Model of the 17th Century

In the 17th century young people who wanted to learn the silver trade were apprenticed to master silversmiths. Through a long term relationship, consistent with a discipleship paradigm, with the silversmith they learned to grow in key skills and attitudes that would distinguish them in their craft. The apprentice's curriculum included spiritual and character growth, skill formation, and how to mentor or apprentice others in the future. These apprenticeship programs were designed to go beyond a *teach a man to fish* paradigm, and also emphasized a *teaching others how to fish* paradigm which was effective in passing on skills, character and knowledge to current and *future* generations. Their challenge was to *observe and deliberately practice* the skills and attitudes of the master. From their first day on the job forward, the master assigned tasks designed to form moral character and key skills in the apprentice, and included sweeping the floor, cleaning the work areas, and making dinner for the master. Skill or competency development in design, smelting and refining of silver, mold making, and silver finishing followed, if, and only if, the apprentice mastered both the attitudes and skills of the early, formative tasks.

Keys for how People Learn

Zenger's[57] work showed that up to 40 percent of all new managers fail in the first 18 months. Hence, organizations who want to promote from within need to start their leadership development from day one. Training someone to be a leader is not a process that happens overnight. It is a slow process that develops with time and experience. "Leadership training doesn't create leaders the very next day. A training program merely provides guidelines for developing people, their visions, and their relationships with others[58]". Leadership development is argued to occur most effectively in the context of real organizational problems with actual personalities. Several large corporations have taken senior management involvement to the next level by having senior officers conduct the training itself. For example, former CEO of PepsiCo[59], Roger Enrico, spent 100 days a year running Pepsi's leadership development program for top management. "The central idea is simple: The most important responsibility of a leader is to personally develop other leaders". Research from the Association for Supervision and Curriculum Development and American Psychological Association demonstrated key principles for learning and development of people over a ten year period. [60] Discipleship methods reflect these key principles of learning which have been proven by extensive research:

1. **People learn what is *personally meaningful* to them.**

2. **Learning is developmental, and *builds upon past learning*.**

3. **Different individuals learn *differently*.**

4. **Much learning occurs through *social interaction*.**

5. **People need *feedback* to learn.**

6. **Successful learning involves *use of strategies*—which themselves are learned.**

7. **A positive emotional climate strengthens learning.**

Here's how:

1. People learn what is *personally meaningful* to them.

Researchers say that learning is most effective when it is "active, goal-directed," and "personally relevant." [61]   People learn when they *want to* learn! Leaders who want to influence the learning of others should attract people to their organizations who have goals which reflect the organization's goals.   The wise leader's methods of recruiting people who were genuinely interested in his mission enabled him to observe and discover the right fishermen who were personally motivated to learn.

2. Learning is developmental, and builds upon past learning.

Adults who have relatively little experience with a topic (novices) typically approach it differently from those who know more about it (experts). If we have played chess or backgammon before, we don't refer to the instructions. A person with no technical training or experience would probably need more concrete, step-by-step instruction as he learned to make a simple engine repair than someone who had more training and experience but was not familiar with the particular engine involved. The wise leader built upon the fishermen's everyday experiences and existing knowledge (farming, fishing, construction) through analogic parables. He then gave them progressively more challenging assignments to build upon their existing learning.

3. Individuals learn differently.

People have different styles of learning- whether by seeing, hearing or doing as explained earlier. The wise leader's show and tell methodology of modeling the skills and attitudes enabled people with all types of learning styles to learn no matter what their learning style was.

4.   Much learning occurs through social interaction.

Because "learning is influenced by social interactions and interpersonal relations[62]", teachers and others who want to promote learning need to pay close attention to the social setting. The watercooler, lunchroom and the hallway have provided great learning opportunities for years. Why? Because the power of creativity and learning goes up incrementally when we can "put our heads together" or "bounce ideas off each other." The wise leader knew this and formed a small community of learners, twelve to be exact, in order to create a rich dialogue and interaction around his teachings among the fishermen. He also sent the fishermen out in pairs so that they would have this community instrument at their disposal to utilize in learning experiences "in the field."

5. People need *feedback* to learn.

One of the benefits of deliberate practice is that, among other things, it provides feedback to learners. Feedback—information from outside regarding the accuracy and relevance of our thoughts and actions—is essential to learning. "Ongoing assessment . . . can provide valuable feedback. The entire system [body, mind, and brain] interacts with and exchanges information with its environment"[63] In teaching speech, one of the most effective methods of helping people learn is to let them watch a video tape of their presentations. This highly accurate and timely feedback enabled the fishermen to recognize and improve their own performance very effectively with feedback from the wise leader through well designed assignments and deliberate practice.

6. Successful learning involves use of strategies—which themselves are learned.

"Learning always involves conscious and unconscious processes" including "thinking and reasoning strategies". For example, people frequently "can learn how to learn" by "sharing aims, planning targets, and reviewing achievement". This critical aspect of self-management is sometimes called metacognition or executive control. To help develop it, people should be coached to think ahead to make sure they have the time and necessary tools for a project and that they have envisioned the steps they will follow to complete it. Then they should be reminded to monitor their own progress as they proceed with the project. The discipleship paradigms entails several different strategies (i.e., modeling, assignments, deliberate practice), that have been demonstrated to enhance both skill and performance over time.

7. A positive emotional climate strengthens learning.

The twin elements of rewards, and personal skill development, provided the fishermen a positive emotional environment that motivated continued persistence in such development. Also, the caring, servant leadership relationship and care which the wise leader demonstrated to his new recruits provides a "greenhouse-like" atmosphere for learning to occur. The recruits knew that the wise leader was "in this for them and their growth and development" so they were motivated to follow him.

What's Next?

For some of you, the lessons and methods provided in this book, are enough for you to "hit the ground running" and begin to change your world. Others, I imagine, may desire further training in these methodologies in order to develop confidence and competence in their understanding and use. The discipleship paradigm is certainly not an easy endeavor. Discipleship is much more demanding than a typical transactional leadership style where the boss, with all authority commands and controls performance, punishing all errant minions. I invite you to visit a new website that is devoted to the advancement and promotion of the discipleship paradigm, www.thediscipleshiplab.com . Here, you will find actual video examples, like the remote control example herein on Meaningful Object Identity, where real people are demonstrating the 7 skills. I firmly believe that the principles that what you have just learned may enable you to change your world. At first, your efforts may seem like a drop of water in a bucket. But over time, like millions of small drops of water in a vast ocean, the condition of our world promises to be dramatically different, thanks to your efforts.

The adventure continues . . .

Stay in touch with the author via:

Facebook: ■facebook.com/donald.doty.9

Website: http://thediscipleshiplab.com/

If you liked The 7 Skills of the Ancient Paradigm of Discipleship, please post a review at Amazon, and let your friends know about this world changing opportunity.

Appendix A

What impact did adult professionals say about how the Discipleship Paradigm affected their leadership skills? How would you rate the contribution of the class to your Leadership on a scale of 1-7 (7 being highest)?

I personally found the class to be extremely helpful in assessing my skills as a communicator, leader, and mentor. In my first webcam experience, Identity, I found I was nervous and not as prepared as I could or should have been. I was not as effective casting my vision as a leader as I would have liked. I feel I could have projected more confidence and spoke more clearly. In the second web cam experience, Modeling, I was able to properly demonstrate how I acquired the necessary information through Providence's information system and then bench mark productivity. I gained confidence and was able to proficiently model and teach an individual properly. I was able to use successfully gather information and utilize humor to help ease tension, and become more relaxed as a leader. 7/7.

How much would I say has the training on vision, modeling, identity, question asking, assignment, storytelling influenced your leadership skills?

My overall experience was very positive. I found through each webcam session I gained confidence and became more at ease with the camera, the individual, and was able to attain the information I wanted. I rate the entire experience a 7 out of 7.

Thank you,

G. O, Swedish Hospital

I would give the training a 7 in terms of added value to in my work life. Both classes contributed to my development in my work leadership style. The readings and assignments in regards to modeling and storytelling also contributed greatly to my learning experience.

K.P.

Director of Branches/North Region| Sound Credit Union

I loved the leadership classes. I felt that the visioning and modeling provided a future state view of how we see and project ourselves. We got the chance to voice and express in a safe and supportive environment. At times this modeling put us in shoes of others and we gained a different perspective from our own. We certainly were a questioning bunch, our comfort with each other broke-down any inhibitions to question just about anything and certainly brought forth healthy and challenging dialog. The up-front modeling for me has always been challenging, I enjoy leading from the rear, my gift has always working to encourage and get the most out of others.

The assignments were engaging and challenging, the leadership exercises were a great way for us to view ourselves. We could see the small little ticks and nuances that we might otherwise be unaware of. The older I become the more I realize how important it is to become a good story-telling. I plan to take more classes following graduation and continue to work on learning art of engaging an audience. Certainly a gift that I have yet to master. On a scale of 1 to 7, I would say this activity was a 6 for me. Great program to provide valuable skills and abilities… like Jimmie said last Monday, we gained and grew from each other and the more we became at ease the greater we became as a group. Thanks for a wonderful experience!

B.R., Esterlline/Kory Solutions

The Leadership Class was eye opening, because it helped me face those areas I was not good in for example being a leader does not mean you always have the answer or the right answer but be willing to listen to those around you and merging the ideas. I was not comfortable with the webcam but I realized I am not comfortable with my physical image so if I use it as a tool to help I will be fine. My overall assessment of the course is a 5 on your scale, I was challenged, blessed, and reassured in many of the topics of study.

J.D.

The leadership class, videos, and assignments changed my perception of how act to others. Our class activities put this at a 7 for how it influenced me. When speaking to others about ideas I am now conscious of how to speak in a way that relates to them. This is because I received criticism from my peers that was honest, and it forced me to breakdown my own barriers and behaviors.
I felt that Leadership Class put me in a position to practice the skills and interact with others. The concept of leadership I feel is distinct is that "Leadership is not something you pursue. It is something others give to you." Leadership Class was effective in real ways.
Cheers,
D.C., Virginia Mason

In regards to leadership skills improvement, I would have to give you a "10" (7 is not high enough). This program, with its emphasis on people, is exactly what I needed. Prior to the cohort, I did not know it, but I was sabotaging myself at work with my own leadership style. Many people at work did not like me, but I did not know why. Looking back, I know why now (I will leave it at that). I transitioned to a new organization about three months into our cohort (January 2011), and I do not have any of the problems that I had at my previous organization. I am actively mentoring a replacement and have built a team of people that genuinely enjoy each other. It now looks like I am going to receive a promotion this summer in which I will go from leading inventory team members for about 1/2 a hospital to leading inventory team members for 9 hospitals. Your tremendous teachings have changed my life and my heart in ways that defy personality assessment probabilities. I am excited to hear from you about the before/after leadership skills assessment that we turned in on Saturday.
J.B., Providence Hospital

I discovered some blind spots about myself. Somehow, seeing yourself on video answers many questions. It's difficult to objectively evaluate yourself but the camera doesn't lie.

The only thing that would have helped me with this process was to have the objectives be presented more clearly. I figured it out after the exercise and felt a bit disappointed that I didn't take more advantage of the opportunity to "practice in front of the camera". Overall I think it was a valuable experience and would rate it a 5 on a 1-7 scale.

S.C., State of Washington

The training provided great feedback on my leadership style and it forced me to become more comfortable in front of others. The assignments helped even in recording them to critique myself and see the obvious flaws that I needed to work on. Furthermore, because of everyone in class seeing and discussing it, it helped me realize other not so obvious things that I could work on. Overall, the assignments were all very beneficial and, even though it is tough seeing yourself on film, I would definitely recommend this as a must in these classes and even other classes outside of the cohort. In my opinion, this has helped in growing my skills of speaking in front of others and helped in being able to accept criticism from the professor and the classmates I worked with throughout.

On a scale of 1 – 7 I would place this activity as a 7.

C. P.

The leadership class were helpful in refining the skills I already possess. As we discussed and practiced the modeling and vision techniques, it reminded me how important it is to convey a clear message and to demonstrate for people when necessary. I have worked for municipalities for 20 years, so my background includes the clear conveyance of policies and procedures to many audiences. The Leadership class refined the skills and ability I currently have. On a scale of 1 to 7, I would rate NU teaching in this area at "7".

D.W.

Deer Creek Water Association

Business Manager

I have approximately 100 people on my team to give you an idea of the size of my team. But I spend approximately 50% of my time on approximately 10 individuals that have the ability to do significantly more.

I have found that leading them in a manner that builds a sustainable culture, that the associates lead and they are the guardrails to developing that culture is one of the best approaches. It delivers empowerment, leadership development, team camaraderie, allows people to be more candid and hopefully lead with humility.

They are the sponsors of that environment and their job is to nudge it.

The more people that know how to do their job and feel empowered to do so, the more likely they will get promoted and have a ready successor to take their place.

R.R., Kroger V.P.

References

1Bass, B. M. (1990). From transactional to transformational leadership: Learning to share the vision. *Organizational Dynamics*, (Winter): 19-31.

Bass, B. M. (1998). *Transformational leadership: Industrial, military, and educational impact*. Mahwah, NJ: Erlbaum.

Bass, B.M. & Avolio, B.J. (Eds.). (1994). *Improving organizational effectiveness through transformational leadership*. Thousand Oaks, CA: Sage Publications.

Gardner, W.L., Cogliser, C.C., Davis, K.M., & Dickens, M.P. (2011). Authentic leadership: A review of the literature and research agenda. *Leadership Quarterly, 22,* 1120-1145.

George, W., & Sims, P. (2007). *True North: Discover your Authentic Leadership*. San Francisco: Jossey Bass

[2] The Essence of Governance In Family Firms – An Insight Into Indian Environment Key. 2014. Singh, Surinder Pal. The First Asian Invitational Conference on Family Business Indian School of Business.

[3] Leader Testimonials and Research design details of the study are provided in the Appendix.

[4] *Servant leadership: A journey into the nature of legitimate power and greatness* (25th anniversary ed.). Greenleaf, R. K. (2002). New York: Paulist Press, 27.

[5] Making People Decisions in the new Global Environment. Fernández-Aráoz, Claudio. *MIT Sloan Management Review,* Fall2007, Vol. 49 Issue 1, p17-20.

[6] Human Resource Replacement Cost: Measures and Usefulness. By: Tang, Tang. *Cost Engineering,* Apr2005, Vol. 47 Issue 4, p16-21,

[7] Behavioral Observations. Sasson, Joseph R.; Austin, John; Alvero, Alicia M.. *Professional Safety,* Apr2007, Vol. 52 Issue 4, p. 26-32.

[8] Assessment of Work Performance (AWP) – development of an instrument. By: Sandqvist, Jan L.; Törnquist, Kristina B.; Henriksson, Chris M.. Work, 2006, Vol. 26 Issue 4, p379-387

[9] Management training: benefits and lost opportunities (part 1). Longenecker, Clinton O.; Fink, Laurence S.. *Industrial & Commercial Training,* 2005, Vol. 37 Issue 1, p25-30.

[10] An Evaluation of Safety Performance Measures for Construction Projects. : Hinze, Jimmie; Godfrey, Raymond. *Journal of Construction Research.*

[11] Thought Leaders' Breakfast Discussion.: Tavis, Anna. *Human Resource Planning,* 2007, Vol. 30 Issue 3, p5-6,

[12] MANAGERS' VIEWS OF HOW TO HIRE: BUILDING BRIDGES BETWEEN SCIENCE AND PRACTICE. Nowicki, Margaret D.; Rosse, Joseph G.. *Journal of Business & Psychology,* Winter2002, Vol. 17 Issue 2, p157-170,

[13] The Future That Has Already Happened, Drucker, Peter F., *Harvard Business Review,* Vol. 75 (Sept.-Oct.), 1997, 20-22.

[14] Examining the relationship between organizational structure, market based rewards and information sharing Tansu, B. (2008). *Review of Business Research,* 8(1).

[15] *The behavior of organisms: An experimental analysis.* Skinner, B. F. (1938). New York: Appleton-Century Company.

[16] Positive reinforcement produced by electrical stimulation of the septal area and other regions of rat brain. Olds, J., & Milner, P. (1954). *Journal of Comparative and Physiological Psychology, 47,* 419–427.

[17] IT Workforce trends: Implications for curriculum and hiring Bullen, Christine V.; Abraham, Thomas; Galup, Stuart. *Communications of AIS,* 2007, Vol. 2007 Issue 20, p 545-554.

[18] Reputation, Goodwill, and Loss: Entering the Employee Training Audit Equation. Clardy, A. (2005). *Human Resource Development Review.* 4: 279-304.

[19] Hire for Attitude, Train for Skill. *Fast Company,* August 1996.

[20] *Social Identifications: A Social Psychology of Intergroup Relations and Group Processes.* London. Hogg, Michael A. and Dominic Abrams. 1988.: Routledge.

[21] *The Boys in the Boat: Nine Americans and Their Epic Quest for Gold at the 1936 Berlin Olympics*

Brown, Daniel James. (2013). Penguin.

[22]*Deep Smarts.* Leonard, D. & Swap, L. (2005). Boston, MA: Harvard Business School Press

[23] Stereotype Performance Boosts: The Impact of Self-Relevance and the manner of Stereotype Activation M Shih, N Ambady, JA Richeson, K Fujita, HM Gray *Journal of Personality and Social Psychology,* 2002.

[24] Identity Dynamics as a Barrier to Organizational Change. McInnes, Pete; Beech, Nic; de Caestecker, Linda; MacIntosh, Robert; Ross, Michael. *International Journal of Public Administration,* 2006, Vol. 29 Issue 12, p1109-1124,

[25] Wooden: J. (1998). *A Lifetime of Observations and Reflections.* (McGraw-Hill).

[26] A Good Clinician and a Caring Person: Longitudinal Faculty Development and the Enhancement of the Human Dimensions of Care Branch, William T. Jr. *Academic Medicine:* January 2009 - Volume 84 - Issue 1 - pp 117-125.

[27] New Survey Shows Greater Concern for Ethical Behavior. Verschoor, Curtis C. *Strategic Finance*, Sept, 2000.

[28] Mirror Neurons. August 12, 2005. Retrieved from http://www.pbs.org/wgbh/nova/sciencenow/3204/01.html .

[29] Leadership development, Krug, J. (1996), *Journal of Management in Engineering*, Vol. 12 No.6, pp.15-16.

[30] Hot new area of brain research offers hope for better training sharper street smarts. (2005). Retrieved from www.forcescience.org/fsinews//hot-new-area-of-brain-research-offers-hope-for-better-training-sharper-street-smarts.

[31] Growing leaders. Hurt, Andrew Christopher & Homan, Scott Robert (2005) *Industrial and Commercial Training,* Vol. 37 (3), 120 - 123.

[32] Stephen Covey interview. *The Costco Connection.* July 1999.

[33] Narrative stories in adult teaching and learning. Rossiter, M. (2002). *Eric Digest.*

[34] *Corporate Legends and Lore: The Power of Storytelling as a Management Tool.* Neuhauser, P. C. . New York: McGraw-Hill, 1993.

[35] *The Book of Virtues,* A Treasury of Great Moral Stories. Bennett, William (1996). Simon and Shuster.

[36] *The Power of the Parables.* Julian, Ron (2003). McKenzie Study Center of Gutenberg College.

[37] New Survey: Majority of Employees Dissatisfied. Adams, S.. 18 May, 2012. *Forbes*

[38] Gallup, Employee Engagement Survey, 2010.

[39] How tomorrow's leaders are learning their stuff leadership can't be taught, but can be learned. Winning companies are creating programs to help people grow Hadijan, Ani. November 27, 1995. *Fortune.*

[40] The development of higher psychological processes. Vygotsky, L.S. (1978). *Mind in society:* Cambridge, MA: Harvard University Press.

[41] *Developing Talent in Young People.* Bloom, B. (1985). New York: Ballantine Books.

[42] The Making of an Expert. Ericsson, A K.; Prietula, M. J.; Cokely, E. T. (2007). *Harvard Business Review.*

[43] *Talent is Overrated: What Really Separated World-class Performers from Everybody Else.* Colvin, G. (2008). Penguin.

[44] Wooden, J.R. (1999). *Practical modern basketball* (3rd ed.). Boston: Allyn and Bacon.

[45] Academic goal orientation and students classroom achievement. Schraw, G. et al. *Contemporary Educational Psychology,* 20 pp. 259- 368. 1995.

[47] Teaching for thinking, of thinking and about thinking. Mctighe, J. (1987). In *Thinking skills instruction: Concepts and Techniques,* M. Heiman and J. Slomainko (Eds.), Berkeley, CA, McCutchan, pp. 11-27.

[48] *Access your Brain's Joy Center.* Sanders, P. (2014). Light Technology.

[49] The Influence of Joy. Solomon, M. *The Journal of Abnormal Psychology, Vol* 12(1), Apr-May, 1917. pp. 70-71.

[50] *Finding Joy in the Journey.* Kurtz, Jaime L., *Journal of Social and Clinical Psychology,* Vol 32(6), Jun, 2013. pp. 700-702.

[51] *The 7 hidden reasons employees leave: How to recognize the subtle signs and act before it's too late.* Branham, L. (2005). New York, NY: Amacom.

[52] Solve the Succession Crisis by Growing Inside-Outside Leaders. Bower, Joseph L.. *Harvard Business Review,* Nov2007, Vol. 85 Issue 11, p 90-96,

[53] Attention-gated reinforcement learning of internal representations for classification. Roelfsema, P. R., and Van Ooyen, A. (2005). *Neural Computation* 17: 2176-2214

[54] *Talent Is Overrated: What Really Separates World-Class Performers from Everybody Else.* Colvin, Geoff. *Portfolio.* October 2008.

[55] Sommer, K. L., & Kulkarni, M. (2012). Does constructive performance feedback improve citizenship intentions and job satisfaction? The roles of perceived opportunities for advancement, respect, and mood. *Human Resource Development Quarterly, 23*(2).

[56] Nolan Ryan on Randy Johnson, 300 wins, and Strasburg. Stone, L. *The Seattle Times.* May 21, 2009.

[57] Zenger, J., Ulrich, D., Smallwood, N. (2000), "The new leadership development", *Training & Development,* Vol. 54 No.3, pp.22-7.

[58] The case for more flexible objectives', Stoneall, L. (1992), *Training & Development.* Vol. 46 No. 8, pp. 67-9.

[59] 'The Pepsi challenge: building a leader-driven organization. 'Tichy, N. and DeRose, C. (1996), , *Training & Development,* Vol. 50 No. 5, pp. 58-66.

[60] *Powerful Learning.* Brandt, Ron, (1998) .Association for Supervision and Curriculum Development,

[61] Caine & Caine. Psychology Review. American Psychological Association. 1997.

[62] Ibid.

[63] Ibid.

Made in the USA
Las Vegas, NV
16 December 2021

38085357R00066